WHAT TO ~~KNOW~~ WHEN

BUYING
a
USED CAR

WHAT TO WATCH OUT FOR

WHEN

BUYING

A

USED CAR

by

Kenneth Salmon

PAPERFRONTS
ELLIOT RIGHT WAY BOOKS
KINGSWOOD, SURREY, U.K.

Typeset in 9½pt Times by One and A Half Graphics, Redhill, Surrey. Made and Printed in Great Britain by Cox & Wyman Ltd., Reading, Berkshire.

DEDICATION

To my family, friends and colleagues with special thanks to
Andrew Kelley, Peter Butler, Julian Richards and
Richard Hawkins.

CONTENTS

1

INTRODUCTION

Buying a used car is a gamble. Buying anything has an element
of risk, let's face it, but a greater element of risk is involved when
purchasing something that has a history, i.e. has been 'used', is
second-hand (or in some cases third or fourth-hand). The guarantees
and warranties associated with buying brand new consumer goods
are forms of insurance — insurance against the goods being
imperfect, substandard, badly manufactured, or breaking-down.
Motor vehicles are consumer goods. Manufacturers assure you that
their products, provided they are professionally maintained and
serviced, should enjoy a trouble-free life and, as a mark of
confidence, provide a warranty to that effect. It's comforting to think
that when anything goes wrong you can simply take it back and
have it repaired or replaced. The original owners of vehicles have
benefited from this insurance/assurance but, of course, they have
had to pay for it.

By buying this book you have expressed an interest in purchasing
someone else's cast-off goods, something that they don't want any
more and something, for them, that has outlived its usefulness.
There are many reasons why you should want to do this. Perhaps
you cannot afford a new car. Perhaps the only new cars you can
afford are cheap and nasty ones and you prefer something a little
better, more comfortable and stylish. Perhaps you need a vehicle
which is to be used for rough and ready purposes and it would be
daft to damage a new one immediately. Perhaps you are a private
individual who cannot benefit from the tax advantages of having
a company car. Perhaps there's a particular model which you really
like that a manufacturer doesn't make any more. Perhaps you refuse
to suffer the tremendous loss in value when a car ceases to be 'new'
and becomes 'used' after having been driven just a few miles home.

Whatever the case, you don't really mind that it has been someone else's possession previously, and I consider that a healthy
attitude which makes good financial sense.

In a Utopian society, where everyone tells the truth and is open and sincere, you would not really need this book. A seller would tell you all you need to know about their car, its little faults and foibles, its history, and any accidents which it has been involved in, why they think it smokes or doesn't start and, in their opinion, whether it will pass its next MOT and the absolutely *genuine* reason why they are selling it. The book might still be of value though as a pointer to any trouble that the sellers are unaware of.

However, we don't live in such a society yet, and not everyone is as honest as they would have you believe. You may be lucky and buy a car from someone who is sincere and will tell you everything about the car — many people are like that. But there's always the possibility of purchasing from a less responsible source or not having the previous owner available for comment. It's best to be on the safe side and to be able to judge a car's merits for yourself to avoid any risk of being 'ripped-off'.

What this book attempts to do is to reduce that risk to the absolute minimum, through the practical application of useful and reliable information. Buying and selling is not an exact science and therefore I cannot guarantee that you will get the best bargain available simply from a careful analysis. It all depends on you, the individual, and how you go about it. But I can guarantee that after reading this book, digesting the facts and using the information contained within, you will save yourself pounds — maybe hundreds of pounds, and depending on the particular price bracket, maybe thousands of pounds.

It has taken me many years of practical research and hard work to gain all this knowledge both professionally and privately. I have been a buyer in the used car market, a buyer of my own private transport, a dealer, a mechanic, and have made very many successful purchases, plus, in the early years, some poor ones. Through this work I have amassed a great deal of knowledge on the subject which I now share with you so that you can benefit from my experience and save yourself a lot of money, money which you might otherwise throw away. I hate to see anyone's hard-earned cash wasted.

2

PRE-PURCHASE CONSIDERATIONS

I don't want to start this book by pre-supposing that you know that the price you pay for a vehicle is not the only cost to be considered. A lot of people overlook or underestimate the peripheral expenses which can, in some cases, amount to double the cost of the purchase of the vehicle. The simple answer is to do your homework. Don't rush in. Ask some preliminary questions before you start looking around. Buying a car is not like buying other consumer goods. If you're buying a fridge there's little else to consider apart from the cost of the item. No-one really sits down and tries to work out if they can afford the electricity it's going to use. You just plug it in and put food in it. When buying a hi-fi, extra costs can be involved, such as a good quality stylus, the records, tapes and compact discs that you're going to play on it. When buying a car there are many other considerations: road tax, insurance, the cost of an MOT each year, running repairs, parts replacement, garage repairs and servicing costs, petrol consumption, installing a radio/cassette, alarm system, attaching a tow bar, parking charges, fines and tickets, membership of the RAC, AA or other breakdown service – and the list goes on and on. All these must be considered, some in more detail than others.

Insurance
It is illegal for anyone to drive on any public highway (road) without being insured against third party risks. If you accidentally smash up your car in a ditch and harm no-one else's property then that's entirely your concern (as long as you were not driving dangerously and recklessly). If you prang someone's wall by skidding on black ice and you were driving carefully then it's a private legal matter and can be settled with a little cash passing between hands by way of compensation. If, however, you were to plough through a jam-

boree of scouts whittling their way along a zebra crossing because
your brakes failed then you're in *real* trouble. The point I wish to
make is that you can be the most careful, sober, considerate and
diligent driver in the world, on the clearest, driest day of the year
but .... there's always the possibility of your brakes failing, a heart-
attack or a nutter in another car or a half-baked pedestrian who
causes you to swerve. If you're not insured then you are taking a
huge risk. In the event of an accident you could be paying damages
for many years and it could ruin your life.

Of course you will want to road-test the vehicle before parting
with a large sum of cash but do make sure that either your existing
insurance policy covers you, you get covered first, or the seller's
insurance covers you. Don't necessarily take their word for it either,
after all they want to *sell* you the vehicle and may exaggerate the
truth a little. It really is not worth driving a car, even around the
corner, without proper insurance. The courts deal with offenders
caught without insurance very severely indeed. You also get a
criminal record.

Road Tax

All cars need to be taxed in order to be driven on the road. The
road fund licence disc shows you have paid the tax. It is an offence
to drive a car on a road without tax. It is even an offence to park
a car on the road without tax, whether you intend to drive it or
not. It is not an offence to possess a car which is parked *off* the
road without tax. You will not receive a criminal record if caught
without tax but the fine may be many times what it would have
cost to pay for it in the first place. Placing a notice stating "Tax
in the post" is simply not good enough and you may still be taken
to court.

Repairs and Servicing

It is rare that after purchasing a used car you will not have to spend
some money by way of repairs or servicing, within the first year
of ownership. The car could possibly be in very good condition
but there may be a few little improvements you wish to make — the
previous owner might not have minded that the wing mirror or aerial
had been vandalised, but it may be important to you.

It is very well worthwhile taking the advice of friends in such
matters, if you do not know a reliable and reputable garage or
mechanic yourself. As in all professions there are good practitioners
and bad. A good recommendation is worth its weight in gold. Do

ask around when considering which garage to take your car to, and so avoid both disappointment and throwing your money away.

It is easy to think that when you make a journey it costs you only the price of the petrol used. Wrong. Every time you drive a car, each and every one of its constituent parts is worn a little bit more. The more they are used the quicker they wear out and eventually need repairing (often it is more economical to replace worn parts completely). Even if you do not drive it for a while it is costing you money in tax, garaging costs, rust damage and depreciation of value over time. Having stated all these extra costs, I hope that you now take them into consideration if you have not already done so. Discount these costs from the money you have available and re-evaluate your purchasing power. Don't leave it until after you start looking, or you could be making a grave mistake.

If you have an older car then it is wise to become a member of one of the motoring organisations (AA, RAC, National Breakdown, etc.). Their back-up service is very useful and, for a small yearly fee, can save you an awful lot of worry and/or inconvenience. It could cost you twice, three times, four times the cost of yearly membership to have your car repaired at a roadside garage or towed off the motorway, never mind the hassle. When you do take out membership make sure to include their optional 'relay' service, which gets you and your vehicle home in case of an accident or a serious mechanical breakdown.

3

THE MARKET

The Yearly Trend

The best time of year to get the best deal buying a used car is most certainly August and September. Many lucky people will be the proud possessors of brand new cars with new registration letters as from August the 1st and the market will be awash with their old trade-ins. New car dealers have too many to handle (more than they know where to park), and have substantial capital sums tied up in trade-in cars, which might be a commodity they do not deal in, and cannot be seen to deal in.

Private individuals who have not traded-in and have bought a new car now have two, one of which they don't want any more. Perhaps they did not want to face a time without the facility of a car and have left it until the new car arrived to sell the old one. They do not want to have the hassle and expense of an extra car which they do not use, they are keen to 'get rid quick'. It is also the time of the year when most people do not want to buy a car. They have returned from their summer holidays and have found that they have overspent, others are saving up for Christmas.

Therefore, at the time in the market of greatest supply there also exists a period of lowest demand (supply and demand being the most important determining factors regarding prices) and we are faced with what is commonly known as a 'buyer's market'. It is over this period that you can select from the greatest range and offer the lowest money and really walk away with a bargain. All sources are affected. The car trader magazines are thicker than usual, the local paper classified ads sections are brimming, the auctions are running longer and later than usual and the used car dealer's lots are parked bumper to bumper.

Conversely, it's the worst time to sell. Buyers are more selective and sellers are pestered by picky people who only have to walk around the corner to look at another similar model. Expect, therefore, the seller to be less appreciative of your call and more reluctant to spend a lot of time with you. Don't be intimidated though and spend as much time examining the car as is necessary.

Regarding dealerships, at this time it's a good idea to ask whether they have any 'un-prepared' part exchange models around the back waiting for space at the front. You might be fortunate enough to drive away a car which may not have the gleam and gloss of the professional manicure but could be the closest thing you'll ever get to a trade price purchase.

There are other seasonal fluctuations: the time leading up to Christmas and shortly thereafter is also a good time to buy (the second best of the year). Late November and December is "shopping frenzy time", therefore "spending frenzy time", and people have less disposable income and are more likely to be in need of selling something to repay their accrued debts. It's also a very cold time of the year and buyers are reluctant to leave their warm comfortable homes by way of public transport. Sellers get fewer calls, fewer offers and are more ready to accept a lower price. Choosing a good time to shop could mean taking notice of the weather conditions and venturing out when others fear to tread.

The worst time of the year to buy are the months of May and June. Humankind has emerged from hibernation once again, savings are at the ready and spring is in the air and in their step. There are maybe three or four times as many inquiries over the telephone for any one car and "hey, anyway, it'll be a nice drive out". Auctions are bathed in sunshine, "so even if there's nothing we want we can get a good tan", and there are more day-trippers passing the flag-draped forecourts. A good summer always sees record sales in the used car market.

So, seasonal fluctuations are important and should be taken into consideration. A change in the weather even can make a whole bunch of difference to your bargain.

There are obviously certain types of vehicle which sell better in winter than in summer. October sees the price of off-road and four-wheel-drive vehicles rocket, and the first hint of spring sunshine sees the sports and convertible market go through the vinyl roof. Even the Met Office is not able to predict the summer and winter in this country, but if you are aware of these trends you can take full advantage of them. The simple rule is to buy these types of cars when it's the worst weather for them — a hot and stuffy four-wheel in mid-summer and a draughty and cold open-top in the depths of winter. Your doctor may not consider it the most sensible thing to do but your accountant will love it. This sort of consideration can save you literally hundreds of pounds.

Types of Car

PRIVATELY OWNED CARS: (which includes saloons, estates and coupés
of varying prices) can often be the best buys. A private car, which
has had one owner from new, may have been looked after very well.
People are often proud of their cars and go to great lengths to
maintain them well. They have often been garaged and therefore
not always subject to Britain's temperate climate. Some could have
been used very rarely, at weekends and evenings only (I know of
one old lady who only used her mint condition Hillman Imp to
go and vote once a year!). Others, of course, can be badly
maintained by people who don't know the first thing about cars and
cannot afford to have them serviced. Generally though, private cars
have done far less mileage than company cars. From a private seller
you will be able to judge how well they have looked after the car
and they will be able to inform you as to its history (i.e. whether
it has been used for towing and hence had a harder life). Prices
can vary; good value from people who undervalue their cars and
don't really know their proper worth, or bad value from people
who are not aware of the massive depreciation which a car is subject
to.

COMPANY CARS: have often clocked up a lot of miles. This means that
nearly all parts of the car have seen a lot of use, from the suspension
to the driver's seat. Many traders try to tell you that "yes, although
it belonged to a company, it was regularly serviced, far more than
if it were a family car". So what! It received regular servicing (if it
actually did — ask to look at its service history) because it *needed*
regular servicing due to its hard life. Companies are not considering
the extended life of the vehicle. After three years or so they don't care
what happens to it.

I don't want you to think that all ex-company cars are bad buys
— they're not — but some of them are. Company cars are sold before
they start to develop faults and become uneconomic to maintain. They
are *not* sold because it would be a nice gesture from a boss to an
employee to give him/her a new car every three years. Business people
don't usually think like that. It is possible that you will pick up an
ex-company car just before all manner of things start to go wrong
with it. Unbeknown to me, a friend of mine purchased a company
car, a four-year-old Vauxhall Cavalier, from a London dealer who gave
her all the chat, "regularly serviced, madam, etc.", for £2,000. Over
the next two years she had to spend £3,000 keeping it on the road!

SPORTS CARS: have usually had a hard life. People often buy sports cars to impress and then proceed to show off in them by driving them fast, burning people off at traffic lights and trying, rather foolishly and falsely, to impress their partners by showing them what their cars will do. You can be lucky and find someone who uses their sports car simply to cruise but, as a general rule, fast cars are bought by people who want to drive fast and do so. Many sports cars are built for such a life and do well from it; some in fact suffer from normal driving. But beware of ordinary saloon or coupé cars with special features that are not really sports cars but are driven as though they were. These cars are often the ones which have suffered from bad treatment. It's not necessarily the fault of the owner but more the manufacturers, who promote these cars as 'sports' when they're not. Don't jump to the conclusion that just because a car has a soft-top, alloy wheels, Recarro seats, spoilers or twin-carburettors that it is a sports car. Also don't believe that if a car is advertised as a sports car in the 'Sports' section of a newspaper or magazine that it deserves to be there. Advertisers normally choose where *they* wish to display their cars and not the publishers. They believe that if they put their coupé in the 'Sports' section it will attract a high price, and it often works. Don't you be fooled by this. For example:

Sports Cars	*Common Misconceptions*
Porsche 944 and 928	Porsche 924
Ford Capri 2.8i	Any other Capri
Sierra Cosworth	Any other Sierra
Triumph TR4 or 5 or 6	Triumph Vitesse or Spitfire
MGA or MGB	MG Midget
Toyota MR2	Toyota Celica
Lancia Stratos	Lancia Beta Coupé
Volkswagon Golf GTi	Volkswagon Scirocco

plus

Jaguar E Type	Dutton
Jaguar C Type	Saab Turbo
TVR 350i	Alfasud Sprint
Lamborghini	MG Metro Turbo
Ferrari	Manta Berlineta
Jaguar XK120, 140, 150	Nissan Silvia

Jaguar XJS V12   a fancy Renault 5
Mercedes SLC   Escort Ghia
Peugeot 205 GTi   Cavalier SRi
Austin Healey 3 Litre   Mini GT
Aston Martin   Fiat X19

PRESTIGE VEHICLES: the luxury end of the market, the BMWs, the
Jaguars, the Mercedes, the Rolls and the Bentleys, the top-of-
the-range Carltons and Granadas, Rovers, Audis and Volvos.
These cars are expensive and are normally made to last longer
than the 'family' type of car, simply because they usually have
larger engines which can take higher mileages. A hundred
thousand mile Cavalier or Escort engine is nearing the end of
its life whereas a hundred thousand mile Mercedes engine could
go on for another 50,000 miles or more. These cars depreciate
in value very rapidly and you can pick up a three or four-year-
old model for a very good price. They're good value-for-money
cars, but the drawback is that they are costly to maintain and
run. They feature many extras, lots of goodies and luxury bits
and pieces which are fun. Be extra careful when choosing these
vehicles because it may cost you an arm and a leg to fix a faulty
component. They must be budgeted for very carefully.

CLASSIC CARS: From time to time there are phenomenal surges in
the classic car market. Such vehicles have become less the domain
of the enthusiast and increasingly more that of the commercial
investor and speculator. This can cause an increase in demand in
a market with a diminishing supply (as cars become the victims
of rust and road accidents, etc.) and can lead to dramatic increases
in prices. Some highly prized 'Collector's Item' cars have been
known to increase in price many times more than the rate of
inflation. Speculators rely on being able to predict the market and
get in before the competition. At times there are peaks, but at other
times prices become more realistic. Do be careful, as it is a market
with increasingly more experienced specialists, who generally know
what they're doing. It needs a lot more detailed and up-to-date
research than any of the other market areas.
Note: Choose a car which is easy to resell, it will therefore hold
its price. There's nothing wrong in buying what is a working tool
and, at the same time, an investment.

4

BUYING PRIVATELY

How to Shop

Take your time. Don't rush in. Don't buy impulsively. I can't stress this enough. Shop around. Whatever you do, don't fall in love at first sight, or you might talk yourself into buying an attractive wreck.

Indeed, it's worth pointing out here that *you* can be your own worst enemy. The dodgy dealer and the fly-by-night cowboy could be your best friends compared with your own emotions. How many times have you bought something and when you've got home thought "why on earth did I buy that rubbish" (or words to that effect). It's no big deal if the item is a cassette or a tie, it didn't cost you that much money. A car, however, will. You must 'switch off' when buying something such as a used car, to avoid being landed with a heap. Think logically and sensibly and use the knowledge gained from this book. To 'switch off' is not the easiest thing in the world — in fact it's very difficult — but you *must* try. Try not to be emotional, otherwise you'll be fighting yourself all the way and will not notice any defects.

Always view with the intention of leaving having wasted your time (and not your money). Don't buy when you're desperate or time is limited — plan ahead. Travel comfortably and conveniently, otherwise you will psychologically be more interested in purchasing. Always view negatively, that is, you should go to look at a car with the view that it has a myriad faults, and you're there to hunt them out.

Newspapers and Magazines — Classified Ads

The first thing to beware of when buying cars privately is that you have fewer legal rights than you do through the trade, if something should go wrong with the car.

The great advantage of buying this way is that you should pay much less than through a dealer, and have more time to inspect a car than at an auction. When searching for a car in this way there is a logical procedure to follow:

1. Do your homework; know as much as possible about your preferred car. If you don't know what you want then look and ask around, make up your mind and then come back to this book. Perhaps you might want to read the notes on the features of the models contained towards the end, and also you may want to do more detailed research at your local library, by buying a book on the particular make or by questioning a local mechanic (for the price of a pint it's well worthwhile).

2. Pop into your local newsagents and enquire as to when the car ad magazines are published (general or specialist, depending on what type of car you want). Set aside that day, or part of that day (or days), for looking for cars and don't arrange anything else. At the same time arrange for a friend who's mechanically minded, if you know one, to be available to see the cars with you.

3. Wait until the mornings that the publications come out and purchase them all, the earlier the better (you want to get to them before anyone else). Many are published on Thursdays in readiness for a good weekend's hunting. You may also choose to purchase a selection of your local and regional newspapers, most of which have a classified used car section. Though there may be only a limited number in each, it is worth your while being aware of *all* the cars that are on the market.

4. Scan through the ads and pick out what you think is a bargain, from what the ad says about the car and the price. Judge as to whether it is a good price (cross reference by using the *How to Value* procedure which follows), circle the ones which you think are bargains and get on the telephone. Don't worry about calling early and disturbing people. Those people who have not got answering machines yet will probably be glad of the interest in their car and won't mind being troubled in the morning. Obviously try not to wake them up, but over breakfast is fine. Sometimes people make it plain in an ad to call at a certain time. Respect their wishes but do make a note to call bang on time, be first on the phone, there may be others chomping at the bit.

    People selling cars often advertise like estate agents. They tend to exaggerate the truth and distort the facts in order to attract you to come and look, in the hope that you fall in love with what you see. It is illegal for anyone to lie in a classified advertisement, if it says "in good condition" it must be in good condition otherwise you have some recourse in law to demand your money back. It is wise, therefore, to retain a copy of the newspaper in which the ad appeared should you purchase the car and something goes wrong which contradicts the advertisement. Estate Agents may describe as a "secluded bijou tree-lined shaded garden" what is in fact a three-square-yard patch of waste ground surrounded by blocks of flats with a dead shrub in the corner. Used car ads can be just as deceiving to the untrained eye. For example:

If it says this :   *it could mean this :*

Good Condition For Age .... Rusty, what do you expect of an old car?

1986 .... expect it to be C reg not a D

C reg .... expect it to be a 1985 model and not 1986

Two good tyres .... Two bad tyres

MOT .... Only a month left before needing a new one

Good engine .... Poor bodywork

Used daily .... Gets me to work and back, just

Service History .... a couple of bills for new tyres and an exhaust

A real eye-catcher .... pink with lime green spots

Recent bills .... lots of things are starting to go wrong

Radio/cassette .... but it doesn't work

Radio/cassette .... Blaupunkt or Alba?

Average mileage   why not just print the mileage?

Needs slight attention... needs £4,000 spending before it works

No offers .... I'll make it sound like a bargain

Runs as new . didn't really run very well when I first bought it

Cloth trim .... seat covers hiding worn upholstery

Diamond alpine shining bright white .... white

Pacific aquamarine .... blue

Metallic paint .... hard to touch-up

A real bargain ...... well, that's my opinion (for all it's worth)

£1,995 .... it won't sound like Two Grand

Not for the fainthearted .... boy-racer's car

Luxury car at a sensible price .... wide-boy's car

Genuine reason for sale ..... it's knackered and I want rid of it

Matching interior .... as bad as the exterior

Four speaker stereo .... but only one works

Owner going abroad .... where you'll never be able to find me

Spoilers ....spoilt it
Very clean ....recently washed
Two owners ....a rally driver and a family of fifteen
Etc, etc, etc ..."

What an advert doesn't tell you could be as important as what it does. It could be that the seller did not want to spend too much on advertising, but it could mean that they are trying to hide something. People rarely advertise a car's bad features but they always promote its good ones. So it is wise to double-check *all* the details of the advert on the telephone. This may save you a lot of wasted time. Also make sure to enquire about all the other facts that they may have missed out. Facts which you will need to be able to judge a good car from a bad one. It's best to make a list of the following twenty questions on a piece of paper, photocopy it, and then fill in the answers for each car. Keep this information for future reference.

Note: When responding to an advert in a newspaper or magazine always say first, as soon as the phone is answered, "I'm enquiring about *the car*." In this way the trader who is pretending to be a private seller and who may have an assorted bag of used cars outside his house, will have to say "Which one?". Another trick these people use is to advertise cars under slightly different names, such as Mr Robert Johnson, Mr Johnson, Johnson, Robert, Rob, Robby, Bob, Bobby, BJ, etc. Then, whichever name you ask for will inform them as to which car you are interested in. Ask to speak to "The person who is selling the car". There are more part-time traders, who pretend not to be traders and masquerade as private individuals, than you would imagine. Perhaps they sell a few cars each week, one a fortnight or a couple a month, but they do so to make a profit. They know that they can attract more clients this way, as the public is wary of used car dealers, and that they will not be subject to the Sale of Goods Act. You can often make as good a purchase from these people as from private individuals, but it is best to know exactly who you are dealing with.

Twenty Questions
i)   How old is the car, what year, what registration letter?
Notes: is it a 1985 or 1986 C reg?

ii)   How many miles has it done?

Notes: the average for a family car is in the region of 10,000 miles per year.

iii)   How long have you had it?
Notes: If not long then the seller could have made a bad purchase and is trying to get rid of it quick, before it breaks down completely.

iv)   How many owners has it had?
Notes: As a general rule the fewer the better. More due care is likely to be paid to the car and more money spent on it if an owner has kept it for a long while.

v)   Is anything wrong with it?
Notes: Be blunt and note the response. It's a fair question, but people tend to avoid this one, they think it rude.

vi)   Does it have a service history?
Notes: preferably a service book which has been stamped at 6,000 or 12,000 mile intervals, bills for repairs and servicing are second best, but if none of the above is available you won't know if it has been well maintained or not.

vii)   What colour is it? (What do you mean by azure?)
Note: Can you live with that colour?

viii)   How long is the MOT?
Notes: It should be at least 6 months or the reason for sale could be that the owner doesn't believe it will pass next time.

ix)   When does the Tax run out (under the present system it costs £100 a year to tax a car)?
Notes: not desperately important but worth money nonetheless.

x)   Which model is it?
Notes: Is it a Base model, an L, G, GLE, GTE, GTi, coupé or saloon, etc.

xi)   Why are you selling it?
Notes: Does the answer sound reasonable or simply made-up?

xii)   Where did you buy it from?
Notes: From a garage, a private seller, a member of the family or an auction?

xiii)   Any warranties or guarantees?
Notes: How long do these last/When do they run out?

xiv)   Any rust, dents, scratches, rips in the upholstery?
Notes: A fair question which may save you time and trouble
viewing the car.

xv)   Has it had any accidents?
Notes: You or anyone before you. In your opinion do you think
it has been hit or has hit anything?

xvi)   Do you mind the car undergoing a professional
examination?
Notes: They shouldn't, they should welcome it. A good test of
character this one.

xvii)   Is the car still subject to any hire purchase repayments or
requirements?
Notes: Be sure that the car is not, since the finance company will
have the right to repossess it.

xviii)   Have you made any specification changes?
Notes: Altered the engine, put twin carbs on, changed the wheels?

xix)   Have you added any extras?
Notes: Does it have rear seat belts, a stereo that works, fins or
spoilers, furry dice?

xx)   Has it been adjusted for lead-free petrol?
Notes: Something all car owners should do immediately they
        purchase a car these days.

These questions are not necessarily in any order of importance
but they're all important, you may have your own priorities. If you
are satisfied with the answer to one then proceed to the next, but
if you are not then politely say that it's not the car for you and don't
waste any more of your or the seller's time. Move on to the next car.

5. Arrange a time to call as soon as conveniently possible. Give
the seller your telephone number, should the seller have to cancel
the date. This might save you time and expense.

6. Then, move on to the next car and, if suitable, arrange a time
with that person as well. Do this for all the cars you have picked
out — you can always call and cancel the appointments should the
first or second car be suitable, but it's always best to guarantee
yourself a selection. In that way you will not force yourself into

an unwise purchase simply because there are no others to choose from.

7. Arrange that your mechanically minded friend can meet you so that you can view the cars together.

8. Don't be late for your appointments or you run the risk of annoying the seller (which you obviously don't want to do).

9. A useful tip is to arrive at your appointed viewing time a little early, maybe fifteen minutes, for private sales. Check the address and where the car is parked and if it is around the corner from the house (as it's not always easy to park outside your own house) you can then take your time examining the exterior of the car before knocking on the door. This will allow you to do some tests that you might prefer not to do under the watchful gaze of the seller. It will also allow you an opportunity to judge whether the car is worth any continued exploration − it could be so full of rust patches that you'd rather not waste any more time than politeness dictates.

10. Remember to make a mental note or write down all that the seller says on the telephone and in person, for future reference (should the car not turn out to be all you were led to believe).

11. Examine the car thoroughly − perform the tests described in the section *Easy Tests,* on page 51.

12. If you are happy with the car then inspect the documents. Make sure the name and address of the seller is that stated on the registration document, otherwise the seller may be a dealer in disguise. If the sellers haven't got the registration documents, *don't buy the car.* It might not be theirs to sell! If the car is more than three years old and they don't have the MOT, then consider that the car hasn't got an MOT or, worse still, it hasn't passed its MOT for some reason. Make sure that a car nearly three years old is not coming up for its first MOT and the reason for sale is that the seller believes that it will not pass. If the car is being sold with a service history or bills for work done, then check all the paperwork. Make sure that you are discussing the deal at the seller's home − gain entrance to the premises if you can, for a cup of tea or the like − otherwise you may have difficulty, if the car goes wrong, getting in touch again. Beware people who wish to meet at your place rather than their home − always go to them.

13. If you're a little dubious about the seller or the details he has

given you, or if the registration document is not in his name or at his address, then call your local police station and express your doubts and politely ask them to run a check for you. It varies from station to station and who you get on the phone as to whether they'll do this for you but it doesn't harm to try and they're usually obliging. They're not allowed to divulge any information other than (a) it is a registered number and (b) whether it is on a stolen vehicle list. This is well worth doing before parting with any money, and the service is free.

14. Haggle over the price. Aim for at least 5% to 10% less than the advertised price, especially when advertised as 'ono', but haggle even if it is not. You'll be surprised how reasonable people will be in order to sell their car and avoid the hassle of having loads of people knock on their door, particularly if they're busy. Haggling is quite an art; it can also be a great deal of fun. It's not very British though. We do tend to consider haggling rather down-market and crude. Well, personally, I'd rather swallow my pride for a few minutes and save myself an awful lot of money than maintain a stiff upper lip and pay a couple of hundred quid for the privilege. It's up to you but haggling is always worth a try. If you don't like the idea then simply calculate 10% below the asking price and offer that to the seller 'take it or leave it' (but much nicer than that). If they don't take it, which they well might not, then you can always pay them what they want for it and still get the car. You don't lose anything by making a good offer, the seller will expect it more often than not. Don't make silly offers though, half-price or a third off, because you'll only offend people.

15. If the offer is accepted then shake hands on the deal and leave a small deposit (perhaps one hundred pounds) as a good faith gesture. It's a little unwise in this day and age to carry lots of cash about your person and, after all, you don't know what the neighbourhood is going to be like. Get a receipt for your deposit and sign a bill of sale of which you must take a copy, or sign two identical ones and take one yourself. Arrange a time to pay the remainder and off you go. You're happy with the deal, the seller's happy with the deal and that's what business should be all about.

16. There follows an example of a bill of sale, which either you or the seller can copy if you wish. Don't necessarily use their idea of a bill of sale if it doesn't contain all that *you* want it to say.

Bill of Sale

Vehicle Details
Car Type and Model   : _____
Registration Number   : _____
Taxed until   : _____
MOT until   : _____
Other details   : _____
(such as radio/cassette,   _____
to be included in price)   _____

The above vehicle is being sold as seen, tested and inspected. The seller has the legal right to sell the vehicle or is entitled to sell it on behalf of the owner and it is not subject to a credit agreement.

_____

Previous Owner Details:
Seller's Name   _____
Seller's Address   _____
                       _____
                       _____
Postcode   _____

New Owner Details:
New Owner's Name   _____
Address   _____
                       _____
                       _____
Post Code   _____

Sold For   _____   pounds   only

Deposit Left   _____   pounds   only
Date   _____
Signed For   Seller _____   Buyer _____

Remainder   _____   pounds   only
Date   _____
Signed For   Seller _____   Buyer _____

_____

How to Pay

1. Personal cheque — the only problem with this method is that the seller will usually require that you wait three working days for the cheque to clear (money to pass from your bank to theirs). If it's a personal cheque from a Building Society account it can take up to ten working days to clear. For a small charge you can apply for 'special clearance' which only takes twenty-four hours through a bank. Check with your bank as to whether they do this.

2. Banker's Draft — usually the safest method of payment and widely accepted as you have to pay cash to the bank to get them to issue you with a draft. However, these days they are easily forged and, again, the seller may want you to wait three working days before picking the car up. If the seller is a little dubious then ask them simply to call the branch where it was issued for confirmation. That may put his mind at rest.

3. Business Cheque — no better or worse than a personal cheque really.

4. Building Society Cheque — roughly the same as a banker's draft where cash is immediately debited from a person's account on issue of the cheque. But again, the recipient may require that you wait until it has cleared into their account. It is a secured form of payment insomuch as it can only be 'stopped' (say if it is stolen or misplaced) by the payee, not the drawer, and therefore can, in effect, be considered as cash. When deposited, cash can usually be drawn against it immediately. However, people do know that these cheques are occasionally stolen from building societies and passed on and they can regard them with suspicion. They know that if they receive such a cheque the society will not honour it. Therefore, I suggest that you ask the seller to telephone the branch at which the cheque was drawn for confirmation of its authenticity. Don't confuse a Building Society Cheque with a personal cheque drawn from a Building Society Account, they're not the same thing at all.

5. Cash — the easiest and the most readily accepted form of payment but also the most dangerous. You will have no record of where the cash was paid in or to whose account (which you might need to trace if something goes wrong). You could easily lose a tightly rolled bunch of notes on the street, which would be disastrous or, even worse, it could be stolen — you could be mugged. If a cheque is stolen it can be stopped. But cash is still the easiest form of payment, so if you are concerned about carrying large sums of cash, how

about this: arrange to meet the seller at the bank and do the business there, in the lobby. Pay in cash in order to get a good low price. There's nothing like a briefcase full of crisp notes to persuade a buyer to be a little more reasonable.

A seller might suggest the following. To pay half in cash (or as much as you feel comfortable carrying about your person) and the rest by personal cheque. Then sign two copies of the Bill of Sale and retain one yourself. Then you take the keys and the car now and he/she holds onto the registration document and MOT until the cheque has cleared, then they send it to you in the post. I wouldn't recommend this way, or any variation on it, it's full of loopholes. Documents can get lost in the post, and if the seller does not know where the MOT was issued you'll have to re-MOT the car. You may need the documents to show to the police (or you may be prosecuted), your insurers, the post office (in order to tax the car). In certain circumstances, if you don't have the documents as well as the Bill of Sale, to support your claim to the car, the seller may accuse you of stealing the thing. It has been known to happen. There are all sorts of reasons why you should simply not enter into this sort of arrangement, it relies too much on trust, on you trusting someone you've never met before.

Always ask for a receipt for a deposit. If you leave a deposit whilst you arrange for a professional inspection then write "deposit subject to inspection" and get the seller to sign it. If the car doesn't pass the inspection you can always then claim your money back.

Note: No matter how short of cash you may be, *never* drive a car if you are in any doubt about the amount of petrol in the tank. Petrol gauges are not known for their accuracy or their longevity. The mechanical part of it (contained within the tank, usually at the back of the boot) often wears out quickly and gauges have a tendency to stick. It takes a while to get to know your car's petrol gauge and a car's petrol consumption. Some cars have reserve tanks and others have a healthy margin between showing 'empty' and running out. But if an older car does run out of petrol it can be pretty serious. Petrol tanks rust and the deposits build up at the bottom. If the deposits get into the engine, via the fuel pipe, they can clog up your carburettor and do enough damage to render that important item useless. It's an expensive replacement. When the tank has petrol in it these deposits are denied access to the fuel pipe by a filter. However, if the car runs out of petrol the resulting pressure created by the engine being starved of fuel can cause these deposits to be sucked into the engine. To avoid the expense of replacement parts rendered useless by petrol tank deposits, simply *do not* ever run out of petrol, think ahead, make a point of filling-up when your guage shows a quarter tank. But always, when you have just bought a car and are driving it home, call into the first petrol station you see and fill up.

Car "Dating"

There are a number of companies around today who advertise in the press and on television as computer data used car sales companies. Basically, you telephone them up and they hold on their computers lists of vehicles which are for sale in your area. For example you can ring up and say "I'm looking for a C registration Ford Escort 1600 L, and I don't want to pay more than £3,500 for it. What do you have?" and the telephonist will reel off a list of the vehicles that they have on file which closely match your requirements. This is a new form of car trading, relatively untested, which I have heard some very strange reports about, few of which have been good, unfortunately. They are expensive to register with and therefore you should expect to have to pay a higher price than you would, say, through the newspaper. People do tend not to inform these agencies once they have sold their cars, so often you can call one of the numbers they give you and be disappointed. Still, it only costs you the price of a phone call for the information, so they're therefore worth a try. Look in your local car trader type newspapers and the Yellow Pages for their phone numbers.

5

HOW TO VALUE

There's an easy and very convenient way of being able to value a particular car; buy one of the Used Car Price Guides from a local newsagent or bookseller (such as W H Smith). These guides (there are a few to choose from) are all pretty similar and generally give the estimated price of relatively recent models of cars (maybe up to ten years old), whether in good, bad or indifferent condition. They are intended to give you an idea as to what to expect to pay. You are expected to judge whether a car is in A1 (showroom), good, fair or poor condition and thus how much it is worth. As their name suggests they are only a *guide*. Because they are convenient they are popular and because they are popular they are considered to be an authority. They are *not* an authority, they are not always accurate and they cannot be completely relied upon. They tend to overvalue.

Having said that, you should buy one immediately. It will serve a purpose.

The best way to judge the value of a car is to judge its *relative* value in the market-place. Market forces are the most important factor in determining price and can be affected by such aspects as time of year, weather, advertising, availability, etc. It's all to do with the economic factors of supply and demand. I have found the following method the best way by far for determining the proper price of a vehicle.

a) Choose which vehicle you want to buy. Let's take a hypothetical example, say you want to buy a Ford Thingumijig, with a two litre engine (2000cc), with luxury features (2000 L), only three years old and with 30,000 miles on the clock, in good condition.

b) Buy (or read at the local library) all the publications available that week which advertise used cars — *The Exchange and Mart*, your regional *Car Trader* magazines, local papers, free papers, used car advert papers, etc. Make sure they are recent and up-to-date.

c) Draw a line down the middle of a sheet of paper and title one column

'Private' and the other 'Dealer'.

d) Take a reading from your Used Car Price Guide for your ideal car. It reads, say £3,500. Put this at the top of both columns. If this is way above what you can afford then perhaps you may have to reappraise your choice. If this price does not knock the wind out of you then proceed.

e) Next, painstakingly go through all the papers for all the cars that are similar to yours and circle them or tear them out. Don't just look for cars which match your ideal description perfectly; also look for similar vehicles, the same make but perhaps a year older or younger or with slightly different specifications.

f) Say you find one that matches your description exactly. It's a private sale and the owner has obviously used his own copy of a Used Car Price Guide and chosen to advertise for "£3,495.00 ono". That's to be expected. Write it down in the 'Private' column.

g) The next car you come across is a dealer ad for an identical car but the price is £3,850, but includes a 12 month warranty on major parts. It's £350 over 'book' (your Guide) price but you may consider the extra money worthwhile for the insurance cover. Write the price down at the top of the column marked 'Dealer'.

h) Next you find one which is the same model, all the same specifications but is a 1986 D registered. It's a little bit younger and is advertised privately for £4,250, but that sounds quite reasonable since it has only 23,000 miles on the clock. Being a year younger it is probably worth £500 more and the 7,000 miles off is worth £200 more. Add these together and deduct them from the price shown and you arrive at a figure which is a fairly accurate estimate of the vehicle's worth in a year's time with additional mileage accounted for — £3,550. Write this down.

i) Do this for all the cars which come close to yours. Add on some money for a younger car, take off for an older car, take off for a higher mileage than average, add on for a lower mileage, take off for a Base model, add on for GLE with extras. You will then have two lists of cars, higher prices generally from dealers and lower prices from private advertisers. To judge how much to take off or to add on use the differences in price between one model and the next in your Price Guide, also the difference in price between A1, Good, Fair and Poor depending on the mileage and condition described in the ad.

j) Add up all the figures in the 'Private' list and divide by the number of items in the list to get an average price. Do the same for the 'Dealer' list. You will now have the average market price (private and trade) which you can use to judge all the adverts by, and decide whether they are good or bad deals.

k) You will also have a more accurate guide as to what price your particular car is worth in the market place, considering supply and demand and the time of the year. Remember that for an 'or nearest offer' or 'ono' car you should expect to pay between 5% and 10% less than the advertised price when you're negotiating.

Note: Now, considering the average of the 'Private' column only, as a matter of interest, compare this figure with the sum in your Used Car Price Guide which indicates the price the 'trade' is prepared to pay for your ideal car. Don't be surprised to find that these two figures are very close indeed. In my experience the average price of a used car in the paper and what it says in a price guide it is worth to the 'trade' are very similar. You must remember, however, that dealers do not use the public Price Guide books — they have their own, and their Guides indicate much lower prices for dealer purchases.

Rather than always following the above procedure, which is rather time-consuming, I often simply refer to this 'trade' figure for an estimate of what a car will fetch in the market place. However, this method is not as accurate as the above procedure, so I would not advise it for a beginner.

6

BUYING FROM
MOTOR AUCTIONS

What are Motor Auctions?

Auctions are *not* for the uninitiated or uninformed. They are fast and furious places where you have little time to examine a car and you cannot examine it fully. Auctions are where the trade buy some of their stock and, consequently, they are full of traders experienced in the business of assessing the quality of cars quickly and accurately.

Auctions are places where you are likely to pick up mutton dressed as lamb. You can, if you know what you're doing, drive away a very good deal indeed (much better than through the classified ads or from dealers) — but you have to be able to sort out the wheat from the horrendous amounts of chaff. *Don't* go in there to buy without knowing anything about how auctions work. That would be like playing poker with transparent cards, unaware of the rules or the odds.

Please remember that for every hundred cars offered for sale at an auction, there will be only a handful that are worth buying. From my experience of these places this is certainly the case. Your challenge is to become so informed about the pros and cons of used cars, that you are able to judge which cars are worth a closer inspection (and possibly worth bidding on) and which must be totally ignored. Do be prepared to admit that there may be nothing at a particular auction worth giving a second thought to, and walk away.

I don't want to put you off auctions as they are marvellous places to find real bargains. What I do want you to beware of are the numerous pitfalls.

The first thing to know is that there are good auctions and there are bad auctions. The good are really good and the bad are absolutely awful and there's very little middle ground. *Do* make

34

sure that you check, on arrival, the auctioneers' Conditions of Sale. They are legally obliged to display this information on their premises, normally in the Sales Office, and you can pick up a copy from the desk. Some auctions can be and are, shall we say, a bit dodgy; indeed some I wouldn't trust as far as I could throw them and neither should you. You're quite safe with the large auction companies (such as ADT or British Car Auctions or Central Motor Auctions and the like) but the waste ground set-ups are to be avoided *at all costs,* and I really mean that. You have to trust your instincts here, what they look like and how they operate — do you trust them? Ask around, ask your friends. Have they had any bad experiences at any particular auction? Look for affiliation of the Society of Motor Auctions (SMA — the nearest you'll get to a guarantee of fair play and honesty).

Check on the Conditions of Sale what the auction house guarantees (seriously, you must do this). For example, if you buy a car and it turns out to be stolen or still under a hire purchase agreement, will you get your money back (your cash normally) without any problems? I know of many people who have bought from auctions cars that were stolen, and which they first had to give back to the proper owner and then fight tooth and nail through the courts in order to get their money back. This is a time-consuming and expensive process, and you're not guaranteed to win.

The law is not on your side at these places; it's as though the courts really don't know what to make of them. You are not covered by the Sale of Goods Act and therefore have to be very careful indeed. Personally, I wouldn't go near an auction that wasn't a member of the SMA, but it's up to you.

What Happens at Auctions?
There are two areas of an auction, one usually open to the elements or partially covered, which is the 'pound' (where cars can be viewed and inspected) and the normally enclosed part, the 'arena' or 'ring', where you will find the auctioneer (where the bidding and buying takes place). Normally a car will have a 'Lot Number' on it and this indicates when it is due to go into the ring. Cars will have tickets on the windscreen which tell you some facts and figures about the car, i.e. whether it has an MOT, how long it lasts, what the car's mileage is and whether it's genuine, the year of manufacture, if it is taxed, etc. The amount of information displayed and the reliability of that information depends entirely on the respectability of the auction house. It is worth noting that the more information that

is given the more credible the auction is likely to be.

Vehicles fall into two distinct categories at auctions: those that are sold *As Seen* and those that are sold *With Warranty*. 'As Seen' means you buy the car with all its faults and problems and you have no recourse whatsoever — if it blows up on the journey home then tough. Buying a car like this is really very silly. There's a reason why the owner of that car has put it in the auction 'as seen' and not with a warranty, most probably because it has a fault that would be detected upon closer inspection, closer than you are allowed at an auction. I don't want to go into too much detail here but simply *don't* buy a car 'as seen' from an auction, unless you really want to gamble against the odds.

Buying a car 'with warranty' means that you normally have an hour after the sale to drive the car around and inspect it thoroughly for faults. Check what 'after sale' means as it could mean after the fall of the hammer, after the auction ends or after you've paid your money and bought the car. Buying a car with a warranty is almost as good as buying a car privately and you will probably have paid less money. If you find a 'major mechanical fault' then you can take the car back and have your money refunded. What constitutes the definition of 'major' varies from auction to auction but you must always argue if you think you have a case. It obviously doesn't mean that you are entitled to a full refund if the windscreen wipers don't work, as that's relatively cheap to fix, or if you simply don't like the car (it's not like at Marks and Spencers). Do double-check the car has a warranty with it before you start bidding.

Cars go into auctions at two levels, those that have a 'reserve' price and those with 'no reserve'. Basically if a car has no reserve price then the highest bidder buys the car on the fall of the hammer, irrespective of whether it fetches a good price or not. This sounds marvellous if it's a cold day and hardly anyone turns up, but, normally 'no reserve' cars are at the lower end of the market, i.e. tatty old bangers which you would be wise to avoid. If the car has a reserve price then you will not be told what that is; it is the auctioneer's and seller's secret. It is the price below which the seller is not prepared to let the car go and may prefer to keep it or sell it privately. If bids go above the reserve price then the car will be sold to the highest bidder. If bids do not reach the reserve, one of two things can happen: either the auctioneer stops trying to raise the bids and lets the car go back into the pound without selling it (where it may be offered at the next auction in a few days' time) or he will sell it 'provisionally'. A provisional sale means that the highest bidder has an opportunity to negotiate, via the telephonist in the office, with the seller, to agree perhaps on a compromise price, somewhere between your highest bid and the reserve. This often happens because people offer their cars at auction for too high a reserve price. This is understandable as the seller obviously wants to get as much money as possible for his vehicle and people all too often consider their car to be worth more than others are actually prepared to pay for it.

Auction Procedure
The best thing you can do, if you're not particularly mechanically minded, is to take someone along with you who knows something about cars.

Whether they or you know about cars, you may not know about auctions. I suggest that you first go as a spectator with no intention of buying. Get to know the feel of the place, how an auction works, the kind of people who attend auctions, differentiate between the dealers and the public and try to tune yourself to the atmosphere of the place. Become aware of the auctioneer's method of presentation, his slang and his speed. Check some cars out, value them and sit and see if they go for what you expect. This exercise is certainly not pointless. It can be very informative and a good deal of fun, particularly if you go with friends. A 'dummy run' could save you a lot of money.

You may detect a slight fault whilst inspecting a car, that's to be expected with any used item. It may just be a slight scratch mark, a bald tyre, a missing wing mirror or a blowing exhaust, which doesn't really detract from the fact that it is still a good car and might go for a good price. It is wise, therefore, to take a notepad and pencil with you to the auction. Write down the Lot Number of the vehicle and next to it jot down any defects that you must take into consideration when judging how much to bid for it. Also note any other facts and figures for your quick reference. This is important because you may get flustered when it comes to bidding and forget these details.

Your note may say:

Lot 45 Ford Granada, 1984/B Reg
one bald tyre, needs new back bumper,
low mileage (24,000), very good condition otherwise,
no tax, year's MOT.

Many people believe that to feign disinterest is the best policy at an auction, because too much attention will push up the price someone else is prepared to pay — it'll make it look a good buy in the eyes of others. Well, from my experience of auctions the contrary is true. The *more* attention you pay to a vehicle the more you will put off the competition. They'll think that you are going to buy the vehicle whatever the price (as some people fall in love with cars). They may give in and look elsewhere at other models. Don't forget that you are forking out a lot of money here and you want to inspect your potential purchase as fully as possible. Intimidate people and look like you've made your mind up — *this* is the car I'm going to buy, so hands off! They don't know that you've carefully set a price above which you are not prepared to go. Fool them. Do your inspection well in advance of the time the vehicle comes in to the arena. Always keep your eye on the car though and make a mental note of others who are looking at it. You'll then be able to pick them out in the arena and know who you are bidding against. Watch for the auction driver and hang around when he starts the car and check on the exhaust smoke (see section on Easy Tests). When the car is in the arena, or about to go in, ask the driver to release the bonnet catch and have a good look at and listen to the engine. Try quickly to perform the tests described in the section 'Easy Tests ...', but do remember that if you buy the car you will have an hour to inspect it fully — if it comes with a warranty.

Good Buys and Bad Buys
Vehicles are offered for sale at auctions for every reason under the sun. The secret of a successful purchase is partly being able to judge the reason, good or bad, why it is being offered for sale.

Some general examples of why vehicles are entered into auctions and whether they are good or bad buys:

POSSIBLE GOOD BUYS:
1. Cars which are repossessions by finance companies who are eager to liquidate their assets quickly.

2. Cars that have been taken as part exchange vehicles by dealers who do not trade in used cars and, likewise, are eager to liquidate their assets quickly.

3. Cars that have been taken as part exchange vehicles by specialist dealers who do not trade in those makes of cars or those models and, likewise, are eager to liquidate their assets quickly.

4. Cars sold by private individuals who need cash quickly.

5. Cars sold by people who think that auctions are places that you get good prices for cars (wrong assumption).

6. Cars sold by people who can't be bothered with people calling at their homes (perhaps famous people, timid people).

7. Demonstration cars that have been used for six months, have perhaps had all their teething troubles sorted out by the garage and have less than 10,000 miles on the clock. Look out for holes in the roof, the bumpers and dull patches on the paintwork where sales and advertising stickers and/or notices have been fixed — these may cause problems later.

POSSIBLE BAD BUYS:

1. High mileage cars which, if advertised, will not attract buyers, offered by companies, rental firms, taxi firms and private individuals alike.

2. Cars that have defects which would be apparent on inspection, or a test drive, but may not show up in the arena of an auction (usually 'as seen' cars).

3. Cars which are starting to develop faults and to cause expensive problems and it is more economic to replace them.

4. Cars which have been seriously damaged and repaired and whose faults would show up on a test drive but are not that obvious idling in a car park and driving slowly through an auction arena.

5. Cars that have lots of bits and pieces wrong with them but no major mechanical faults.

6. Cars sold by Police, Council, Water and Electricity companies, and other large organisations.

7. Cars which have been written off and put back together.

Bidding

Bidding at an auction is one big game. If you want to win the game then you have to know the rules. It would be helpful to know a little of the special language used by the auctioneers which is understood by (and for the benefit of) the dealers. Prior to bidding the auctioneer may subtly suggest to the dealers what the reserve price is. If the reserve price is £2,000 he may say "Well, ladies and gentlemen, where shall we start? How about two thousand?

No, okay then, let's start at fifteen, you tell me." If the auctioneer considers the reserve price too high he may deduct a hundred and suggest that. If too low he may say "It's here to be sold". When the bidding has gone above the reserve he may suggest this and say "It's all your own money now, folks" or "I'll take a chance and put it on sale", when he's not really taking a chance at all — he's not allowed to.

Try to keep a low profile and not let any opponent see whom they are bidding against. Mingle with the crowd and don't stand apart. Don't throw your hand in the air and shout. Attract the attention of the auctioneer through eye contact or by the slight wave of a hand, he'll then know you're in the bidding and keep looking back at you for a bid. Once his attention has been gained you can bid through a slight nod of the head which, in a crowd of people, is very difficult to detect. If another bidder cannot see whom he is bidding against, he may believe that the auctioneer is accepting false bids in order to raise the price and mistakenly give up the ghost. You might benefit from this by eliminating the competition. Whether taking false bids can be considered fair-play or not is of no consequence, neither is whether it's still practised. The important consideration is that people *believe* that it exists and you can use this to your advantage.

Set the price that you are willing to pay for the car before bidding commences (its value you will have assessed earlier), and don't go above it. *Don't* get carried away by the excitement of the game. You're bound to be nervous, after all you are parting with a lot of hard-earned cash, and in nervy situations we are all prone to becoming a little illogical. Convince yourself that the car is not worth buying over and above a certain price and stick to it (see chapter 5, *How To Value* on page 31).

Don't join the bidding until the last minute, if possible. If a car is still at a reasonable price, jump in towards the end and put the competition off their guard. Consider it a fun game in which you are trying to outsmart your opponent. Wait until the auctioneer is in the process of saying "going once" or raising his hammer before you jump in. You may cause all sorts of disruption, so use this technique to the full. Make sure the auctioneer can see you when you jump into the bidding. He/she will usually only take two bidders at a time and may not look around for anyone else until one person has dropped out, so don't feel that you're being ignored.

An auctioneer will generally expect a private individual to pay more for a vehicle than a trader. The auctioneer can be in control

of the price of a car and it is therefore advisable not to be easily
distinguished as 'Joe Public'. I'm certainly not suggesting that you
carry a cellphone, a copy of the latest trader's car price manual
(Glass's Guide or Black Book) or, wear a sheepskin coat and bulky
gold accessories, but do try to appear a little difficult to categorise.

Payment

If your bid has been successful then you will have to go to the
rostrum immediately and pay a deposit of probably 10% of the
purchase price (this percentage varies from auction to auction).
Before you start bidding make sure that (a) you have checked with
the office as to the exact percentage they require and (b) you have
the cash on you. Auctions do not take lightly to someone who wins
a bid and hasn't got the cash. You're wasting their time and they
may ban you from any future proceedings.

The most accepted methods of payment at an auction, unless
you're a trader, are cash and banker's draft. You're normally
expected to pay for a car within 24 hours of winning a bid, otherwise
you could become liable to pay a daily parking fee while your cheque
clears (three working days). Make sure that before you bid on a
car you have the money readily available to pay for it.

Dealers' Tricks

Dealers love to put the uninitiated off buying cars at auctions,
particularly cars which they themselves have an eye on. They
generally dislike the public at auctions as private individuals can
push up the price of a good car to a value beyond that which a dealer
is prepared to pay (if he is to make a decent profit). They may do
this in a number of ways. A common one is to engage in
conversation. This establishes your trust in them, and they then go
on to talk about the merits of the car which you're considering
bidding for. They'll tell you all the things that 'an expert' can see
wrong with it and that you, being a mere novice, are obviously
unaware of. You're unaware of the problem normally because there
isn't one – he's making it up to put you off. It's basic human
psychology to believe that someone else knows more about a subject
than you do, we're generally humble and unassuming creatures.
Used car dealers have not normally followed this evolutionary
pattern. *Don't* always believe that if someone *looks* like and *sounds*
like they're an expert that they necessarily are one. Very often you
are as good a judge of a vehicle as a dealer is (especially if you
have digested all the facts in this book). Of course it is wrong

of me to suggest that everyone who may talk to you at an auction has an ulterior motive. They may be really good guys trying to give you a piece of worthwhile advice. In general though I would suggest that you don't take anyone's advice unless you know them.

There are certain tell-tale signs which suggest that a car belongs to a private seller and not a dealer. It is important to know these, as you normally get a better deal from the former than the latter. Look for the dealer's trick of spraying the hub-caps silver and using liquid rubber to brighten up the tyres (a tacky and sure-fire giveaway which doesn't fool anyone nowadays). Look in the engine for a recently sprayed (black) radiator cowling. Look and smell the cockpit for the use of lacquer. Look for new carpets in the boot and the floor of the cabin, gleaming chrome and paintwork.

It has been known, at less credible and reliable auction houses, for 'plants' to be found in the crowd. Just as you will be trying *not* to look like 'Joe Public' these people are employed by the auctioneer to *be* 'Joe Public', to blend in with everyone else. It is their job to pump up the bids on certain cars, perhaps cars which the auctioneer is having trouble selling and have been through the arena many times before. You could find yourself bidding against someone who has no intention whatsoever of actually buying a car. Even if the ploy fails and all the bidders drop out, and the auctioneer has to sell the car to the 'plant' he's lost nothing. The auctioneer will simply bring the same car in the next day and try again. This is not a widely practised tactic, but it has been known to exist (it's as unscrupulous as loaded dice) and unfortunately is extremely difficult to spot. But seeing as you are a sensible individual and will have set the price you're willing to pay for a car, and *won't* go above that, it is unlikely that you will be taken in in this way.

Conclusion

You can avoid many of the pitfalls that others may well fall into at an auction by following the steps detailed throughout this book − by examining a car properly and being able to judge its worth accurately.

The final word on auctions must always be that whatever you do *don't, don't, don't ever* buy a car from outside an auction on the street. These cars are stolen more often than not and you'll lose all your money to some common criminal.

To find a selection of auction houses near to you consult both the Yellow Pages and your Used Car Price Guide.

7

BUYING FROM THE TRADE

Used Car Dealers

As there are numerous sources when buying privately, so there are when buying from the trade. Some are good and some are bad.

Firstly, there is the waste ground dealer. Anyone can sell cars, as long as a certain code of practice is followed (roughly) and you've got a bit of money. Anyone can set themselves up as an 'Arthur Daly' on a piece of waste ground, perhaps using a portacabin as an office. There are no professional qualifications necessary or exams to pass. These are the people to be wary of, unless you really do know what you are doing and can take along a good qualified mechanic (note: there are qualified mechanics and there are *good* qualified mechanics).

Secondly, there are the more established larger used car dealerships with huge forecourts, proper heated offices and carpeted foyers. The people who own these establishments most probably started on a patch of waste ground and have worked their way up!

Thirdly, there are the franchised new and used car dealerships, perhaps specialising in one or two particular types of car (Audi and Volkswagon, Peugeot and Renault, etc.). The main difference from those previously mentioned is that these are often regulated externally, they may be controlled by the main dealers, the suppliers, and have sales quotas put on them and all sorts of other stipulations. The sales people at these places often work on a commission basis (what they earn is based on a percentage of their sales), so they are very often more professional, more highly trained but also more aggressive and clever at manipulating people. They are trained in sales psychology and understand the dilemma we all go through in decision-making when buying such an important thing as a car. They know how to push and prod, question and answer, to make us persuade ourselves that we want to buy that particular car. It may not have been the car we intended to buy.

It may not be the car most suited for our purposes. We may even have simply called into the garage to ask directions, but we end up buying a car.

Fourthly, there are the classified adverts with 'Trade' or 'T' at the bottom of them. These are usually one-man operations buying from the trade, or from auctions, and selling to the public. They usually give you some sort of guarantee with the car they sell to you (check how long it lasts and what it covers) and their prices are often more competitive, simply because they have lower overheads (maybe they operate from home).

Springing up all over the country now are these Car Supermarkets. Large warehouse-type places filled to capacity with loads of cars of every kind on every floor. The problem with these set-ups is that there may be all sorts of hidden extras put on the top of the price (number plates, tax, delivery, etc.). Also they don't specialise in a particular make or type.

But wherever you see a car you desire and you wish to inquire there are certain things you need to understand.

First impressions are very important. Trust your instincts here. If the sales person who comes and greets you looks a bit dodgy and sharkish or the place you've walked into appears shabby and dirty then be wary. If they don't care about their appearance or their work-place then they probably won't care about what they sell or the quality of their service.

Look around for a dealership which displays a sign to the effect that they are members of the Motor Agents Association, the Scottish Motor Agents Association and/or the Society of Motor Manufacturers and Traders. These organisations operate a code of practice which members are expected to observe, and regular checks and inspections are made. They offer protection for a customer, whereby if a complaint is made, an arbitration and conciliation board can rule on the matter. Also note whether the dealer displays any motoring organisation badges (AA or RAC) who inspect a premises before recommending them.

Used car dealers obtain their stock from much the same sources that you can get them from, only they offer them to you for a higher price (which is their profit). Some are part exchange vehicles from new car dealerships who perhaps don't deal in used cars. Some are bought from auctions. Others may be bought from the public, some may come en mass from companies where they have outlived their usefulness, others may be unpopular models sold straight from the manufacturer.

A sales person's job is to sell cars. This may seem perfectly obvious and not worth stating, but the most recent sales technique to be employed is to appear relaxed and friendly, pretending that the last thing that he/she wants to do is to pressure you into buying a car. Don't be fooled. It may be clever and very subtle but they're still trying to flog you a car. The techniques are many and varied. I shall describe a few so you know what to be wary of but my best advice is to (a) make sure before you consider buying that you know exactly what you're after (b) look and test for yourself (using the information contained in this book) and (c) only use the sales person for information that you wish to obtain and don't be taken in by all their waffle and patter.

Sales Techniques
Do not give away too much information as to what kind of person you are, what you're after, what you can afford, what you need a car for or how you intend to pay for it. It is not necessary for a sales person to know very much about you at all but they will want to know everything. The only person who needs to be party to this information is you and you alone. The more a sales person knows about you the more chance he will have of using your hopes and desires as a weapon against you. A sales person may ask you all sorts of questions that on the surface appear innocent and just friendly chat. In reality they all have a subtext. A sales person is not interested in passing the time of day, only selling cars, his time is his money. He may ask you, for example, "What kind of car are you driving at the moment?", as you can often tell a lot about a person from what they drive (whether they're economy-minded, a bit sporty, safety-conscious, after reliability, etc.). If he can get this information out of you he can show you towards the kinds of cars you might buy and not waste time exploring the other makes and models. If he finds out that you've a family, then he'll conclude that you're more likely to plump for a Volvo than an MG and begin to highlight the safety aspects of the car, the rear seat belts, the crumple zones, the reliable brakes, etc. He may ask you how much you can afford, though he probably won't say it in this way, more likely "What is your budget?", or something similar. Well, this is simply none of his business and avoid answering by retorting "I'm after a good deal, that's all". The questions are too numerous to mention. Just be careful and play your cards close to your chest.

Questions	and their real	*Meanings*
When are you looking to buy?	Can I sell you a car today?	
Are you to part exchange?	Am I going to be landed with a wreck?	
Is it a company purchase?	Is it your money, or someone else's?	
Are you looking elsewhere?	What competition am I up against?	
Have you bought here before?	Are you happy with our service?	
The paperwork	The contract	
Your authorisation	Your signature	

If the salesman tries to talk jargon or tries to baffle you with science then simply ask him to talk simply. Whatever you do, don't give them your address or telephone number, or you'll be pestered by pseudo-friendly calls inquiring whether you've bought yet or not, and when you're coming back to look, or that they've just got in the *right* car for you. How do they know what the *right* car for you is?

Also please do not sign *anything* before reading the conditions carefully.

Another dealers' trick is to start filling out forms in front of you, presuming that you're going to buy. By playing on your inability to refuse point blank or your guilt over wasting their time, they may get you to sign for something you really don't want. Ask them, "What are you doing? What are you writing?" and simply say "I don't want to do that." They may be a little more subtle than this. Beware of questions such as "When would you like the car delivered?" or "Are you going to be in on Tuesday?" which pre-supposes that you want it and forces you to say "I don't want it!", which a lot of people find difficult to say — we consider it rude. Well, consider the sales person rude to jump to conclusions in the first place.

Procedure

Find someone who is well recommended by friends (perhaps where they look to buy cars). Personal recommendations can be very helpful.

Always visit first without any intention *whatsoever* of buying. Go first and use the exercise as a fact-finding mission, an opportunity for you to help yourself decide which type of car most suits your needs.

Don't presume that, because a car is being sold by what looks like an established and bona fide dealer, the car has been thoroughly checked and is in good condition. Perform all the tests like you would if you were buying privately. Always insist on a test drive (a dealer will normally have insurance to cover you).

Oh, and do remember, car dealers may be a little lenient with their own MOT tests, though they could risk losing their licence if they are. It is worth emphasising here that MOT certificates should *not* be considered the gospel proof of a roadworthy and safety-satisfactory vehicle.

Part Exchanges

A dealer may not want to take your old wreck off your hands because it will cause him hassle — he'll have to get rid of it somehow and probably won't make any extra money out of you. Indeed it's more of a gamble for him, he may even lose money on the deal. Don't be amazed then when a dealer grumbles about the idea or simply doesn't want to entertain it.

If the dealer will accept it (and be pushy here, force it on him if you have to) he'll try to pay as little for it as possible. You, obviously, want to get as much for it as possible. Be reasonable, and try to negotiate a fair price. A dealer will assess the value of your old car by using two sources of information. First, he will look at and inspect the car in much the same way as you will his. Secondly he will refer to his authority on the subject, his Glass's Guide or Cap Guide or Black Book. These books are updated regularly and contain professional assessments of the 'trade' prices of used cars. They are not available to the general public — we have to rely on a Parker's Guide (or similar, available at newsagents). The sources available to us are not as reliable or accurate as the sources available to the dealer.

On a general inspection a dealer will assess your car by considering the following:

1) Is it a good, saleable (in demand) colour? Black, white and red cars sell better than green, brown, cream or yellow cars.

2) Is it a saleable model? An L, GL or GTi model will sell better than a basic or 'base' model. A convertible will sell better in the spring than the summer, and a four-wheel drive vehicle better as winter approaches. Although when new, estates and automatics are more expensive, they have, surprisingly, lower used resale values.

3) Does it have any attractive extras? For example a sunroof, electric windows, a good stereo, and increasingly nowadays, rear seatbelts.

4) Is it a 1986 C reg or a 1985 C reg?

5) Does it have a low or high mileage?

6) And after all these have been taken into consideration is the car in good, bad or indifferent condition?

To judge whether you are being offered a good or a bad price, assess the value of your own car beforehand, being as objective as possible, as you would over your prospective purchase. This also helps you if a dealer won't tell you how much he will give you for it, but instead asks you "How much do you want for it?"

If the dealer doesn't want it then all is not lost, you can either sell it privately (where you will probably get a better price) or, if you don't want the hassle of that, sell it to another dealer (one of those 'Used Cars Bought for Cash' places, though again shop around). Even if the car has just failed its MOT and is a complete wreck I wouldn't recommend you get rid of it to a scrapyard. You won't get a lot for it and you'd probably get much more if you offer it in the papers as 'for spares or repair'. Scrap dealers have not got rich by offering wads for knackered cars. You will only get a few pounds if you're lucky, nothing at all if they have to collect it.

The law — when buying from dealers — says in essence: the car must be (a) of merchantable quality (fit for its purpose of getting you from A to B); (b) as described in any advertisement; (c) reasonably fit for the purpose *you* tell the dealer you want it for, e.g. for long journeys or carrying heavy loads. Any warranty or guarantee is in addition to these basic rights.

Dealers are not responsible for any faults that they tell you about. The dealer is also not responsible for any faults that should have been revealed when you or an expert inspected it. If you find faults on an inspection then get the dealer to reduce his price.

If you have a problem? Demand to see the manager.

Seek the advice of the trade associations (for addresses see chapter 14 on How to Complain, page 109). They have a code of practice which is designed to protect you.

Warranties and Guarantees
These are normally the insurance policies taken out with the dealer against the vehicle breaking down just after he's sold it to you. What

you really must check is precisely what the warranty covers, how long it lasts and, sometimes, what does it specifically exclude. Make sure it's in the form of an insurance policy or it could well be worthless. Some are offered by the manufacturers, but don't jump to the conclusion that they are perfectly kosher. Again, check them out carefully. Some policies cover mechanical problems but exclude electrical ones and various parts. Some have a clause built in whereby you have to pay the first 10% of the claim or the first £50 or something like that, to discourage you from making a claim.

Credit

Car dealers usually employ a 'Finance Manager', otherwise called the 'Finance Consultant', or 'Business Manager'. Whatever their particular area of expertise, you should nevertheless regard this person as an insurance sales person or credit broker. It is his job to sell you an insurance policy and finance terms, both of which you simply may not require, need or be able to afford. They also work on a commission basis and can be very persuasive.

If the Finance Officer/Manager/Consultant or even the sales person tries to interest you in any credit terms be very careful, whether it is in the form of hire purchase terms or in the form of a loan. If you are thinking of borrowing the money to pay for your used car then *shop around*. The world is full of organisations desperate to lend you cash and their terms are becoming more and more competitive. There may be a cheaper deal through your bank or building society than anything a dealer could offer you.

The most important aspect of credit is the *APR* or Annual Percentage Rate — basically how much the companies charge you in interest per year. The lower the APR the better the deal. Assess what the borrowing will cost you (including any 'credit insurance' which you may wish to take out to cover you in the event of illness or unemployment). Most dealers can arrange credit but you don't have to accept their offer. You can always leave a deposit on a car while you shop around (but do remember that if you don't buy that car you will no doubt lose your deposit).

One benefit of a credit package tied to a car, rather than a loan from a bank, could be the ability to seek the help of the credit company if the car develops a problem, and the dealer is unsympathetic or goes bankrupt.

A dealer isn't usually going to be too pushy about offering you his particular form of credit. They don't make too much money out of it and it's often not worth their while spending lots of time on the subject.

Insurance

A dealer may encourage you to consider insurance policies which they can offer − motor accident insurance, insurance against ill-health or redundancy against credit agreements, etc. You don't have to accept his offer, and again, shop around, use the yellow pages and the phone, ask the advice of friends, or call into your high street broker who may be able to shop around on your behalf for the best price.

8

EASY TESTS YOU CAN PERFORM

Do be careful when testing a car. It's not yours yet and you're not at liberty to be belligerent, aggressive or over enthusiastic in your tests, prods, pokes and pushes. You may cause damage to the car which you would most likely be liable for. None of the tests which I have described below should cause any damage to a car if due care and respect is exercised. Remember that the car is someone else's property. It doesn't harm to ask the permission of the owner before you begin and, if possible, make sure you have a witness to their acquiescence.

Before performing any of the following tests take a good look round the car and get an impression of the overall general condition.

Assess whether it's been well looked after or treated badly (it doesn't matter if a car has a high mileage or it is very old, as long as it's been looked after properly). Does it sit properly or tilt to one side or to the back? The bumpers should be parallel to the ground on a level surface assuming no tyres are flat). Has it been 'done up' in readiness for you coming round? Is the colour as advertised or is the "eye-catching jade" in fact a horrendous lime green? Ask yourself whether you can live with this car. Is it what you expected, and, providing everything is in order, do you want to own it? If it is not what you expected or not in the condition advertised then politely excuse yourself, walk away and move on to the next. If it looks okay then carry out *all* the following inspection tests.

Before you start, here is a list of items which you might find very useful when going to look at, inspect and buy a car.

Things to take along

1. Magnet — for checking where filler has been used on metal bodied cars.

2. An old handkerchief or larger cloth — to kneel on whilst inspecting the underneath, to wrap the magnet in (so as not to scratch the

paintwork) and to wipe the oil off the dipstick before taking an accurate reading.

3. Torch — for inspecting the engine and underneath the car (particularly useful at dusk, in a garage or at night — though I would never advise anyone to inspect a car in anything other than daylight).

4. Small wire brush — for getting rid of dirt and rust when inspecting wheel arches, exhaust pipe and sills.

5. A Car Price Guide — for quick approximate valuations.

6. A note book and pen — for jotting down faults, features and details (invaluable at auctions) and what the seller has said about the car (for possible future reference).

7. Nail-file or piece of fine sandpaper — for cleaning points and plugs.

8. Screwdrivers — one medium ordinary shape and one medium-sized posi-drive shape.

9. Pair of pliers — to re-attach loose wires that may have 'fallen off' in the engine or to repair a bad connection.

10. This book.

11. One of your friends, preferably one who knows more about cars than you do (if you don't know much), for an objective second opinion, moral support and advice, and as a witness to anything the seller may say to you about the car which may turn out to be false.

12. A gallon of petrol — you may be miles from a garage that is open, and people don't often sell their cars with full tanks.

13. A set of Jump Leads — the batteries even on brand new cars have been known to drain of energy when stood for a long period of time, and you can easily tire a battery out when performing many mechanical tests.

14. Foot Pump — even new tyres will drain of air if stood for lengthy periods, and can render the car unsafe to drive.

15. Spare fuses, bulbs, etc. — a general assortment may come in handy, especially for older cars.

The seller may be able to lend you many of these items, but don't rely on that. Lots of people simply don't know one end of their car from the other and don't keep tools or do repairs themselves.

Exterior (The Bodywork)

It is always best to inspect a car in daylight and in dry conditions. Darkness makes it difficult to have a proper look around and rain serves to make the paintwork look brighter and flashier than it really is. Rain also covers many paintwork defects. Make sure that the sellers have not parked the vehicle near to a wall or fence. They could be trying to restrict your capacity to have a good look. Ask them politely to move the car into a more suitable position.

1. Have a good look around the car and see whether there are any major dints, dents or defects of any nature, and whether they will need urgent attention. Look for body panels which are fitted badly or look a little out-of-joint, as this could suggest accident damage.

2. Look for patches of rust bubbling underneath the paint surface (it may have already broken through in some places). If it has, then it's probably going to break through in a lot more places very shortly. Rust travels upwards, generally, as water collects at the bottom, so start your inspection down below and work your way towards the roof. You can replace the engine in a car for a small fortune but the entire body — that needs a big fortune! If rust has taken a good hold then consider it a terminal cancer. There may be nothing you can do to stop it slowly eating the car away. Rust at the edges of panels and where a little paint may have been scratched off is not a major problem, and you can cure it by using a rust treatment. If rust exists in the centre of panels, in the roof, under all the wheel arches and around the glasswork then it is probably beyond repair already. Check for rust in the following places: around the light fittings, under the front and back bumper, around the edges of the boot and door panels, on the top of the wings, around the aerial, around the wing mirrors, around the wheel arches, basically around the edges of all the panels, where panels join and anywhere where something sticks out of the bodywork.

3. Look at the paintwork, and the colour, and judge whether it is easy to touch-up (metallic paint is very awkward to match). Any scratches or patches of rust in the middle of panels will be much harder to repair than at the edges. Look at the general finish of the paintwork

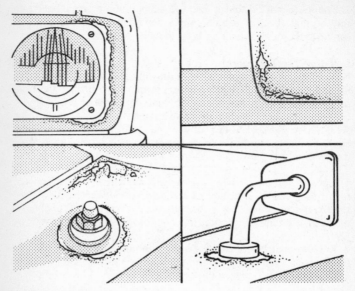

Fig. 1   Likely places for rust.
Top left: Around the light fittings.
Top right: Around the edges of door panels.
Bottom left: On top of the wings, especially around aerials.
Bottom right: Around the wing mirrors on older models.

and see if it is beginning to suffer from the weather and lose its bloom. Ask yourself whether the car has been resprayed (it could be full of rust underneath the paint). The term used for a bad respray is 'blown', which accurately describes how the job was done, with little consideration for the future life of the car. *Gently* press the bodywork in a number of random places with your thumb and see if you can hear cracks under the surface or it feels spongy (rust). To judge if it has been resprayed look under the wheel arches for spray paint over the dirt or on the tyres. Paint which has run over the rubber mountings or the chrome or the glass is a clear giveaway as is different coloured paint under the floor carpets. If the car has been sprayed in damp conditions there will be a whiteness to areas of the paintwork, which is under the skin and impossible to get rid of. A cratered or pock-marked effect (like the surface of an orange) means the paint

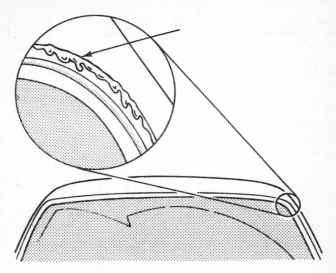

Fig. 2 How to judge if it has been resprayed.

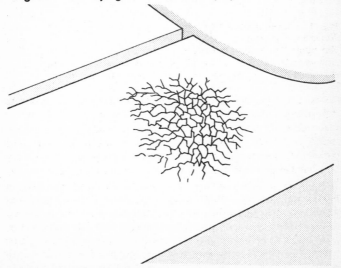

Fig. 3 A ''crazy-paving'' effect.

has been applied too closely. A "crazy-paving" effect means that either
the wrong paint has been used, the surface has not been prepared
properly or not enough time has been allowed for the paint to dry
between coats. All these are signs of a cheap and amateurish job which
won't last long. Don't jump to the conclusion that if you find one of
these tell-tale signs the whole car has been resprayed, it could just
be one section which may have sustained some accident damage.
These areas will usually appear brighter than the other panels
surrounding them.

Fig. 4   Looking underneath the door for rust.

4. Open all the doors and run your hand under the bottom of them
(very carefully — sharp metalwork). Water runs down the insides of
doors, collects and causes corrosion. Then look underneath for rust
(scrape off the dirt with your screwdriver). Any holes here can be
repaired by filler, as this area is not load-bearing and not part of the
MOT inspection. The appearance of rust here will also mean that rust
will have started to eat away at the bottom of the outer door skins and
will eventually show through, if it hasn't already.

5. If the car is security coded — that is, its registration number is indelibly marked on each window — check that the number corresponds to the number plate, front and back.

6. When viewing the overall look of the car did you notice that it looked twisted in any way? This would indicate that the car has had a serious knock which may have affected the chassis. Double check your suspicions by taking a close look at the wear of the front tyres. If they're worn on one side, it could be simply due to tracking, but it could have a much more serious implication. It is worth pointing out here that you should always consider the more serious implication in any particular circumstance to be the case, and only dismiss it when eliminated (i.e. guilty unless proven innocent).

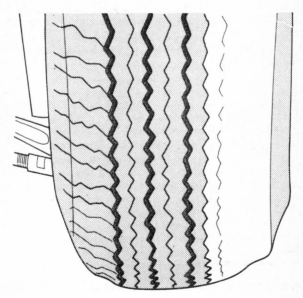

Fig. 5 Tyre worn on one side.

7. Check that all the doors, boot and bonnet fit properly and that they go in to their corresponding holes easily and comfortably. If not, they may have been damaged and attended to (poorly) or replaced altogether.

8. Particularly check the corners of vehicles for accident damage and repair work, as people often misjudge the length and breadth of their vehicles.

9. Take out your screwdriver and check under the wheel arches for serious rust damage. This area is hammered by stones and grit, water, salt and ice throughout the year. Although most cars are well protected, it doesn't last forever. It only takes one flake of paint to fall off for rust to start developing and eat away underneath any protection. Dirt collects here and traps moisture which accelerates the rusting process, so prise it off with your screwdriver and check underneath, push with your thumb, feel for any 'give' and listen for cracks.

10. Check that the windscreen has not sustained any cracks or chips which will weaken its strength. It can be expensive to replace properly. If it does need replacing, make sure you choose a professional. Many bad jobs result in water leakage which causes rot of the floor panels.

Engine

Do be careful when you are attempting to perform the following test that you do not put your hands on places where they are likely to be harmed. For example, avoid going anywhere near the cooling fan, any moving belts, the hot exhaust manifold, or touching both battery terminals at once with a screwdriver etc. (nasty shock). Do not bend over a running engine, allowing any loose article of clothing to hang down (tie, scarf, or even your hair) which may catch in the mechanism and cause you to make a nasty mess of yourself over someone's nice, clean engine. Do not smoke near an engine; you could ignite petrol fumes.

Make sure you check under the bonnet both before the test drive (when cold) and afterwards (when hot) as many problems (especially fluid leaks) show up immediately after use.

1. When you open the bonnet, take a look around again and get a general impression as to the overall condition. There's bound to be oil about, so expect it (particularly on older cars), but an engine compartment covered in oil suggests there's an oil leak somewhere which bodes ill. If it's very dirty it suggests that the engine has not been looked after very well, and that could be a real problem. If there is no dirt anywhere and the engine gleams like a new pin, even though it has gone 50,000 miles, it most probably has been

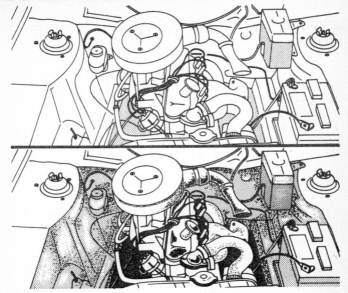

Fig. 6 *Top:* A shiny clean engine compartment.
Bottom: A dirty engine compartment.

subjected to a steam clean. This is unfortunate as the process removes many of the signs which suggest leaks.

2. Pull out the oil dipstick and inspect it. You will probably need to wipe it, re-insert, and then withdraw it again to see properly what it portrays. Check for lots of bubbles in the oil which indicate that the cylinder head gasket has gone or is going. Check the level, but make sure the car is not on a slope otherwise you will get an inaccurate reading. The level should be somewhere between the maximum and minimum marks. If it is too low then it would suggest that the car has not been looked after, and driving a car with not enough (or too much) oil can damage the engine seriously. Whilst you're checking the level also check the condition of the oil itself. Oil does not last forever and should be changed at each major service. It should be translucent and golden in colour, if new (like thin treacle) and dirtier and blacker when used (like thin black treacle). It should never be in such a condition that you can't even see the dipstick through the oil.

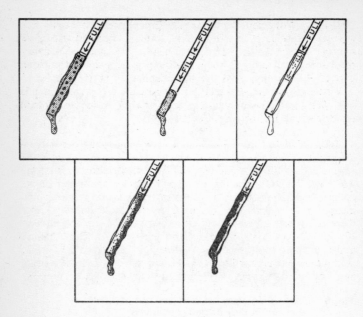

Fig. 7   Inspecting the dipstick.
Top left: Bubbles in the oil.
Top middle: Oil level too low.
Top right: New (translucent) oil.
Bottom left: Used oil, somewhat dirtier and blacker.
Bottom right: Really dirty oil.

3. Whilst the engine is cold (and check that it is before you do this, or you could suffer a nasty burn) take off the radiator cap and look at the water. If there's not enough water then suspect that there may be a leak in the system.

Stick your finger down the hole and look for traces of oil in the water and rub two fingers together. If it feels slimy you can assume that, again, the cylinder head gasket (expensive to replace) is going. If your finger comes out white and fluffy then it has already blown (or there's something seriously wrong with your finger). In wintertime the engine should have an adequate quantity of anti-freeze in the water cooling system (check). This substance lowers the freezing point of the water in the cooling system and ensures that the engine is not harmed by the water freezing and expanding.

Anti-freeze will colour the water blue, green, or in some cases red. A rusty cooling system will turn the water orange and will cause damage to the water pump, the heater and internal radiator mechanism, any alloy castings and the pipes in which it is being carried — basically, most things it touches.

Whatever you do *don't* take off the radiator cap if the engine is hot. Water in the cooling system gets very hot indeed and is then under a great deal of pressure.

4. Take off the oil filler cap and check for any white deposits on the cap itself and the surround, which would suggest water in the engine and a blowing cylinder head gasket. Also do this after the test drive and check that there isn't an excessive amount of smoke coming from the filler hole while the engine ticks over, which would mean a worn engine. Put your hand over the hole and check that there is a gentle breeze passing through your fingers at tick-over. If it blows like a gale then the piston rings may be worn. Always make sure that you get a car warm enough to thin the oil. Thick, cold oil covers up a multitude of sins and prevents any noise being made by worn bearings and the like.

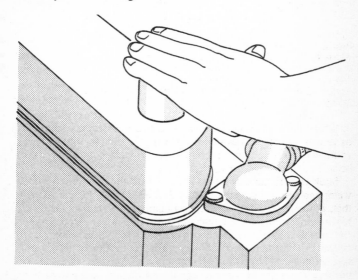

Fig. 8   Put your hand over the hole.

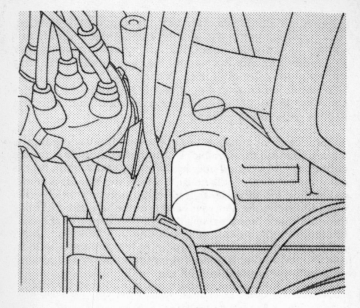

Fig. 9   The oil filter (a fairly brightly coloured object).

5. Look for new and shiny parts (consider this a bonus).

6. There should be at least one fairly brightly coloured object, in what, at first light appears to be a mess of dirty misshapen bits and pieces. This is the oil filter. To be found towards the bottom of the engine on one side. This filter should be replaced as regularly as the oil. If it is covered in dirt and rusty (!) then service has been neglected.

7. Look around the thermostat housing (usually the point at which the top radiator hose joins with the cylinder head) for a makeshift or new looking gasket (cardboard looking thing sandwiched at the point where they join) which could mean the car is overheating and the thermostat has been removed (find out why). Overheating could be due to a blocked water cooling system, an inefficient water pump or a blown (or blowing) cylinder head gasket, all of which are problems that could be expensive to rectify.

An easy test to check the effectiveness of a thermostat is simply

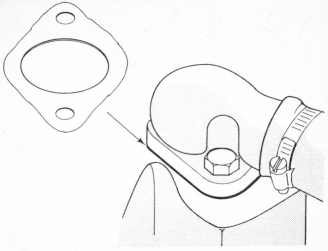

Fig. 10 The thermostat housing — looking for the gasket.
Inset: A makeshift gasket.

to boil it on the cooker in a pan of water. When cold the valve will
be tight shut, when hot full open.

Fig. 11 Defaced engine and body number.

8. Check that the engine and body numbers have not been erased
(and later that they correspond with the details on the registration
document). The numbers are usually stamped on the engine block
and on the body in the engine compartment, where they can be
easily seen. They may be covered in dirt so use your old hanky
and your torch here.

9. Start the engine. If there's a very loud metallic rattling sound at the start (which may disappear when warm) then suspect that the big or small end is going (can be very expensive). But you must be sure where the noise is coming from. If it's from the centre or the bottom of the engine then it could be the ends, but if it's at the front, it could be a simple-to-fix design fault such as a worn cam shaft or belt (OHC). Let the engine just tick over (low revs) and listen hard. A low rumble from the centre again indicates big end wear. Constant knocks and/or rattles can be attributed to timing chains, timing chain tensioner, badly set, loose or worn tappets. A loud horrible noise doesn't necessarily mean there's a major problem. You have to know where the sound is coming from to be able to judge accurately, which isn't easy.

A very useful tip and trick is to carry with you a large screwdriver and use it as a doctor would a stethoscope. Place the sharp end on various parts of the engine (rocker cover, cylinder head, engine block, petrol pump, cam belt housing, etc.) and press the blunt end firmly to your ear. You'll be amazed how easily you can pin-point exactly where a noise is coming from using this method. But keep yourself, your screwdriver and your clothing well clear of moving parts and the high-voltage ignition system. Remember not only that radiators, hoses and engine parts may be scalding hot; electric fans do come on *after* the engine is stopped, as well as intermittently while it is running.

10. Check the battery. Take off one of the filler caps on the top and check the distilled water level. It should come to just above the metallic elements you can see. These days new batteries are often 'sealed for life' and you don't have to worry about the levels. Check the terminals for signs of corrosion (white powdery deposits) which will impair the battery's operation.

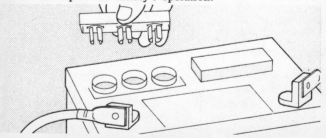

Fig. 12   Checking the distilled water level.

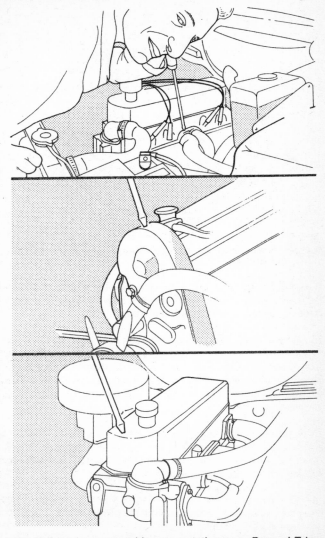

Fig. 13 Using a large screwdriver as a stethoscope. Beware! Take extreme care not to let the blade touch the high voltage ignition system e.g. plug leads.

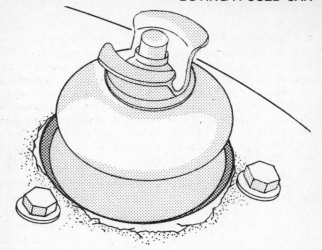

Fig. 14   Rust around the tops of the suspension strut/shock absorbers.

11. Check the inner panels (panels covering the wheels, found under the bonnet) for rust and welding work (especially around the tops of the suspension strut/shock absorbers).

12. Take a good look around for any leaks, or signs of leaks, emanating from any of the fluid pipes; leaks of hydraulic fluid, petrol (you'll be able to smell this) or oil. Check the thicker pipes (water pipes) for water leakage and also for rusty orange stains anywhere where these pipes join the engine and radiator, which is a clear giveaway of a leak.

13. A rattling sound from the front end of the engine could mean a worn timing chain or cam belt (not expensive). A regular knocking noise may indicate that the main crankshaft bearing, or a water pump bearing, or an alternator bearing is going.

14. With the engine ticking over observe whether the entire engine complex rocks or bounces excessively. Such movement suggests split or weak engine mounts.

Underneath
If you can jack the car up do so, if you can't it's no big deal –

most of these checks you can do lying on your back, or kneeling, and looking with the aid of a torch. Often the jacking points on a car are the first to rot away so be careful. Don't rely on the jack (ever) to hold the car up. Always, after having jacked the car up, support the weight by placing wooden blocks (or metal ramps) under the chassis at its highest points. A jack is provided solely for changing a wheel and not to enable you to crawl underneath. Never, under any circumstances, use bricks or stones. They have a tendency to crumble. If a car falls on you, you may be crushed. Be careful not to touch the exhaust, the sump pan or bottom of the radiator if the car has been running recently, they get very hot indeed.

1. Tap the inner and outer sills (the parts of the car which run directly underneath the bottom of the doors) to detect rust. It can be expensive to have new ones fitted, particularly on cars where the sills bear a lot of the weight. If all is healthy the sound should be solid, resonant and deep. Rusty sills often cause a car to fail its MOT. Check, with your magnet, that the sills have not been repaired by filler, which is not advisable as they need to be solid and strong. Look for joins and welding patches. Sills often collect water and rot away from the inside out, so any patches of rust you find most probably go all the way through. Push the rusty patches with your thumb and listen for cracks or any movement. Push *firmly* but not too hard or your thumb may go through which could cause you some pain.

2. Look underneath the engine for bends or crumples in the sub-frame (the thick, solid metalwork which holds the engine in place) which would indicate crash damage. Check that filler has not been used on any structurally important parts which could prove dangerous (and is, incidentally, illegal). Whilst you're down there, getting dirty and damp, check the tyres all round for their general condition.

3. Check for leaking brake pipes, hoses and drums, oil leaks from under the engine and the petrol tank, leaking shock absorbers, any patches of fresh fluid on the road, the exhaust silencer condition and rusty suspension springs.

4. The part of the car which holds everything else together and bears the entire weight of the structure is the chassis. It is, therefore, very strong. Even Samson had his weakness though, and a chassis, made

of steel, does rot eventually. It is usually this which consigns a car to the scrap heap. All manner of other bits and pieces of a car can be welded on and cut off, snapped on and snapped off, replaced and re-replaced. Indeed the entire car can be rebuilt on top of the chassis, but when the chassis is done the car is done. It is imperative then, that you buy a car that has a decent chassis, above all other considerations. Life wasn't made to be a whole bowl of cherries though, and it won't surprise you to learn that the chassis is probably the most difficult part of the car to see, get at and assess the quality of. There are, however, checks you can make relatively easily and quickly.

5. To protect a car underneath manufacturers use what is called 'underseal', a matt black rubber solution which is painted or sprayed on and is designed to resist corrosion for many years, a lifetime some say (though their definition of a life and mine differ somewhat). Salt, used on the road in icy conditions, gets through the underseal via cracks and chips caused by continual attack by rocks and stones thrown up by the wheels. Use your torch and check

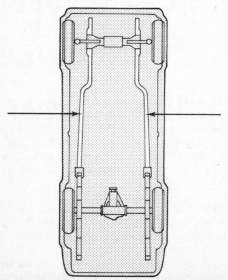

Fig. 15 Looking up at the chassis from underneath the car. The arrows indicate the boxed sections.

the box sections (thick rectangular tubing) for rust (which will appear brown against the black). If you can reach, knock these sections and listen for any sound other than a healthy solid and deep resonance. Water can get into the hollow box sections and rust them through from the inside out. All may look well but you will not be able to tell unless you hit them and poke around a little. Check for any repair work to these box sections. They cannot be bodged with filler, they have to be welded (use your magnet if you can). Are there areas that appear to have been painted recently with substances such as underseal or stone chip guard? Regard these with suspicion, they could have been used to cover up nasty patches, bends or crumples.

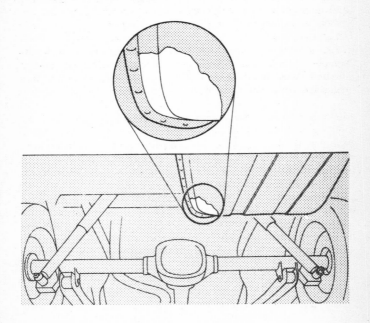

Fig. 16 Petrol leaking from the petrol tank.

6. The thin pipes leading from each rear wheel to the front of the car are the hydraulic brake pipes. Check for rusting and wear. During operation the fluid in the pipes is under high pressure and if leakage occurs the braking system fails.

7. Look at the petrol tank. If you're unsure which is the tank and which is part of the body then tap it with your screwdriver. It'll make a hollow sound, hollower than any other. It shouldn't be too clean, no cleaner than the rest of the car (unless it has been replaced). Petrol is a remarkable cleaning agent, sometimes used to smarten up an engine as an oil solvent (not recommended, by the way). If the tank is leaking, petrol on its way to the ground will clear away any deposits and expose the metal or paintwork of the tank itself. Tanks rot easily, so do look out for this; not only could it be costly but it might cause an explosion.

8. A pipe carries the petrol from the tank to the engine. It's usually thicker than the brake pipes, sometimes opaque plastic and sometimes covered in nylon. Check this for leaks (clean bits again) and any restrictions (where the pipe is bent or caught).

9. Check all the fasteners which hold all these pipes on to the underbody. They have a tendency to loosen and fall off through vibration. Lots of cars have bits and pieces hanging down from underneath, including the exhaust.

10. Check the exhaust for general overall condition and especially rust on the silencer boxes (cylindrical drums, maybe one, two or three, depending on the size of the car) and parts which interconnect with each other. As some exhausts come in parts (front, middle and back), one can be replaced without the other(s). Check over the whole length of the car and don't take one area as representive of the lot (use your screwdriver and wire brush for inspection). If you come across a car with an aluminium exhaust then you're in luck; these things last for many years and if it is one that replaced the original, it is a sign that the owner has maintained the car with a view to its future life. (Also see the section 'Exhaust' on page 77 for tests when not underneath the car).

11. Make sure that any freshly applied dirt, especially under the wheel arches, has not been put there to cover holes and patches of rust.

Interior
Although it is relatively easy to respray a car and make it look gleaming, glossy and new-looking it is not so easy to brighten up a dull interior, especially the upholstery. A car begins to show signs of wear at about 40,000 miles. Look for general wear and tear — rips in the seats, worn carpets, loose fittings, screws missing, tears in the

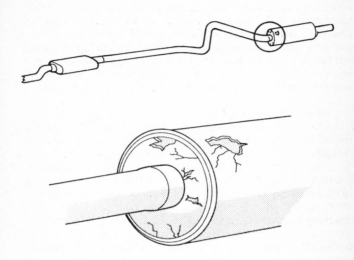

Fig. 17 Rust on the exhaust silencer box.

roof lining, a well worn gearknob (perhaps with the numbers fading).

1. The seats are an important consideration in the interior. Not just how comfy they are (although do test them, because you'll be spending an awful lot of time sitting in them) but also inspect them for wear and tear. This will indicate to you whether the car has been used and abused and even whether the wear corresponds to the mileage shown. Check whether the driver's seat moves forward and back. Take off any seat covers which may have been put there for show, or to cover cigarette burns, loose stitching or excessive signs of wear. Sit in the driver's seat, turn the ignition on (not the engine though) and check that the following work.

2. Check that the warning lights come on with the ignition. Some newer cars have spectacular displays second only to the illuminations at Blackpool, but there are only two or three worth careful attention (the others are really just goodies).

a) Pay special attention to the red (usually) oil warning light (it may say 'oil' or have the figure of an oil can or dipstick) which should come on as the engine is started, and go off after a second or so. When the engine is running it should not come on. If it doesn't come on *at all*, immediately look under the bonnet to see if the wire has been disconnected, to cover a fault. It is designed to light up when the oil level is not sufficient to lubricate the engine's moving parts adequately. Without enough oil the engine will overheat and parts will wear out. The oil warning light works on pressure, it is, therefore, a pressure gauge. If it lights, then there is either too much or too little pressure. This could simply be due to too much or too little oil in the sump, a minor problem. Check the dipstick. If there appears to be an adequate amount of oil in the sump (registering somewhere in between the high and low marks on the dipstick) and the light remains on, then this suggests an oil pressure problem, perhaps caused by crankshaft bearings or a blowing cylinder head gasket (both of which are expensive to repair).

b) If the red (nearly always) ignition light (may say 'ign' or have a figure like a battery) comes on when the engine is running either the battery or the alternator is faulty, or there's a short circuit somewhere.

c) Most new cars are made with brake warning lights as standard (a circle with arcs around it, sometimes red, sometimes yellow), one for the handbrake (lit if engaged) and one for the footbrake. If the footbrake warning light comes on or flickers, then the brake fluid in the reservoir is low and needs refilling. The only reason for this is a leak in the system. Not only can this be costly to repair but it's very dangerous. A seal or pipe could give way whilst you're hurtling down the motorway and then you'll have no brakes and be unable to stop. Some modern cars have sensors on the brake pads which send signals to the driver (light on the dashboard) if the linings are worn dangerously low.

3. Test that the side lights, head lights (both beams), head light flasher and the indicators work (you might have to get in and out for this one if you don't take a friend).

4. Check that the washers and wipers work (front and back).

5. Check that the stereo/cassette works (not too vital).

6. Operate the horn.

7. Pull and push anything else that has a knob or a switch.

8. Look at the carpets. Their appearance is not important as they can be replaced fairly cheaply. Take up any rubber mats which may have been put there to hide signs of wear (excessive wear does indicate usage though).

Look underneath for rot. The floor panels often rot from the inside out, due to rain-water leaking in past worn rubber door seals. Rotten floors can be welded together quite cheaply but it's the reason why they are rotten that's more important, especially if you're viewing on a fine, dry day. The car could turn out to be more use as an aquarium than a means of transport. Another sign of water getting in is rotten, rather than worn, carpets. Look and smell (fusty and mouldy odour, particularly prevalent in old cars).

9. Look at the mileometer and try to judge if it has been "clocked" (turned back). You can usually tell if the wear of other parts of the interior (seats, pedal rubbers, carpets) does not correspond with the mileage shown. Dodgy dealers tend to "clock" a car too much to be believed, such as turning back a 100,000 mile car to 20,000 miles. Contrary to popular belief, it is well known in the trade that this is not done by using an electric drill connected to the speedometer cable.

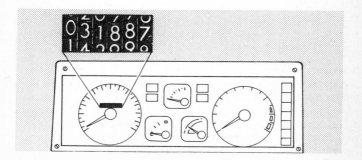

Fig. 18 Has the mileometer been "clocked"?

It's done by removing the instrument facia and mechanically (perhaps with a screwdriver) turning the thousand figure against its rachet. These people leave clues. Look for scratches by the figures under the facia, numbers which are out of line (only half showing), worn screws holding the facia in − these are clear giveaways. A dealer does not have to guarantee the mileage of a car, but if he does not believe the mileage to be correct he must say so. It is estimated that one in four used cars in the UK have been "clocked".

10. Get out of the car, open the boot and check the condition of the spare tyre. Also check whether the car comes complete with wheel brace, jack and tool-kit. Whilst doing this, look around the tips of the rear suspension mounts for evidence of corrosion.

Fig. 19   Corrosion of the rear suspension mounts, usually visible from inside the boot or behind the back seat.

Steering
Stand outside the car and through the driver's window turn the steering wheel from one extreme to the other. The wheel in front of you should react positively and immediately. If there is any play in the system it could indicate a need to replace the universal joint or ball joints, steering rack or box, very expensive. If the steering is operating efficiently there should be no play at all, it should be taut and the wheel should immediately turn the wheels.

With Power Steering, switch on the engine and again turn the wheel from one extreme to the other. Listen for any grinding noises which indicate wear. There should be no loss of power and the

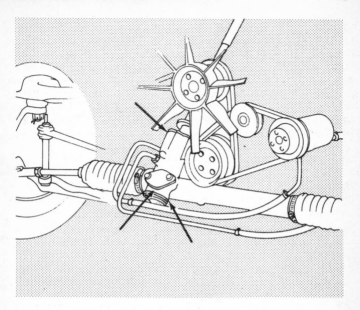

Fig. 20 Check for leaks from the power steering unit.

engine should not stall (but you can expect a slight increase in noise when at full lock as the pump is doing a lot of work at this point).

It is not easy to 'feel' the road with power steeering, and it becomes far more difficult, if play exists, to control the car in a skid. Remember that, if the engine should fail whilst in motion, so does the power steering and it can become almost impossible to steer. Replacing a power steering box can be an expensive process. Check that there are no leaks of fluid from the power steering unit or its pipes or connections. The unit runs from a pulley and is mounted at the side of the engine (often well hidden) and a thick pipe or pipes transfers the fluid under pressure to the steering rack. Inspect all the seals and joints at each end of the pipes as well as the pipes themselves.

Shock Absorbers
Bounce the car, by pushing down above each wheel individually and firmly, watch and listen. Listen for any sound of a hissing

noise during the movement, this indicates air getting into the system and therefore decreasing its efficiency. If the shocks are working properly all round the car, they should return to a steady position after one or two bounces. If the car continues to wobble like a jelly then replacement may be necessary. They are not expensive to replace and can be fitted at a specialist centre. Do make a mental note that shocks cannot be replaced independently. They *must* be done in pairs across the car or the handling of the car will be affected tremendously. When test driving, observe that no knocking noises come from the area of the shocks as this will indicate worn or loose suspension mountings.

Brakes
To test the brakes, press the pedal down hard and keep it there with continued pressure. It should stay put. If it moves after the initial push, then there is a leak in the system somewhere. When on the test drive, and on a clear bit of level road, brake carefully. If the brakes are in alignment, the car should pull up straight and not tend to swerve or even move to one side. Try to do this in such a place so that the car will not be affected by any side wind (which might give you a false impression), and also be careful not to go too fast; twenty to thirty miles an hour is quite adequate.

The same problems with servo-assisted brakes exist as with power steering, in that when the ignition cuts out (should it for some reason do so) then you partly lose control of your brakes.

To check the efficiency of the servo system (power assisted braking unit), if the car has one, perform the following test. Sit in the driver's seat and with the engine turned off apply the handbrake (also make sure the gears are in neutral). Press the footbrake pedal down hard and pump a few times. Keep your foot down and start the engine. If the servo is working efficiently, the pedal, under your foot, should 'give', that is, it should depress. If it doesn't 'give', then the system is not operating properly (which can be expensive to repair, since the whole unit will have to be taken apart, and, perhaps, replaced). Release the pedal and depress once more. The operation of the pedal should be positive. It should feel like you're squashing a tennis ball under your foot. It should not be too solid (squashing a golf ball) or, more importantly, too light (an egg). Repeat this test, just to make sure.

Handbrake
If the car is parked on a steep slope then it is easy to test the

efficiency of the handbrake without starting the engine. Simply engage the handbrake, depress the clutch (if in gear) and see if the car moves. If it isn't parked on a considerable slope then start the engine, engage the handbrake and try to move away on low acceleration. If the handbrake is working at its potential, it should stop the car going anywhere.

Exhaust

Listen, look and smell. Listen for a popping noise emanating from underneath the car, indicating a hole in the exhaust system. A low grumbling sound (like a racing car) when the car is being revved suggests the same, or that an exhaust bracket has shaken loose. Look under the car and see if the exhaust is old and rusty or has any smoke coming out in any other places than the hole at the back end. Grab the exhaust (when cold) with your hand and shake it gently. If it feels firm and doesn't rattle or knock, then you'll know that all the mountings and brackets are there and working.

If you experience a smoky or gassy smell inside the car while the car is running, then exhaust fumes could be finding their way out of a hole and into the interior (which isn't very healthy). Replacing an exhaust isn't cheap but costs vary depending on the type of car. It's usually a quick process at a specialist centre nowadays, found in most towns. Aluminium exhausts, though much more expensive, last a long time, as they do not corrode.

Check the emissions from the exhaust (from the hole in the end) which can tell you a lot about an engine. A good engine, when warm, should not produce any visible smoke, though a *little* is to be expected in an old car (but only when cold). Black or blue smoke indicates piston ring wear, white smoke a blowing cylinder head gasket. Do expect white/grey neutral smoke, more like steam (which it is) if the car is cold and it is damp. Moisture in the air condenses in a cold engine and the exhaust itself; it evaporates when heated.

If a car blows out smoke when started from cold and the smoke stops after a few revolutions, then suspect worn valve guides, which are allowing oil to seep into the cylinders when standing.

Start the car and place your hand about six inches away from the exhaust outlet. Leave it there for a few seconds and then have a look at your palm and smell it. There should be no fluid deposits on your hand, other than perhaps a little dirty water when cold (condensation). There should be no oil and certainly no un-burnt petrol. Oil deposits suggest worn piston rings, which are allowing the engine oil to pass into and through the cylinder chamber and out through the exhaust. Petrol deposits suggest a cylinder which is not firing all the time (usually accompanied by the occasional 'backfire'). This may be simply due to a dirty or worn spark plug, but could be a result of poor compression which, again, suggests piston ring wear (very expensive problem).

Gearbox

Sit in the driver's seat and, without starting the engine, depress the clutch and check whether the stick goes into all gears easily and smoothly. Start the engine and do the same. With the engine still running, check that the gearstick does not excessively vibrate, which is a sign of wear. The easiest gear to test is first gear. To test the gearbox and the synchromesh, put the car in reverse and drive slowly backwards a short way. Brake carefully, and as the car is *just* coming to a standstill change into first gear. If you find it difficult or it makes a grinding noise, then this suggests a tired and worn gearbox (which is an expensive item to repair/replace on all makes of car). Some older cars may not have synchromesh on first and reverse gears (which allows you to select those gears whilst in motion). In which case, you will have to change from reverse into second gear. Please do be careful when you do this. Only perform the test at very, very slow speeds and very carefully. You do not want to be accused of damaging someone's car. If performed with diligence and at a snail's pace, you will be fine.

Automatic Transmission

When the transmission changes gear automatically, it should be smooth and silent. The engine should not over rev before the changes take place. Most have a semi-automatic facility (gears 1 and 2) and you should check them on the test drive. Simply use them to change up and down and observe if they respond quickly. You can test the majority of automatic transmissions as follows: Stop the car, keep the engine running, engage the handbrake fully, also use your left foot to hold the footbrake on. With the car locked in position, and with no obstacle immediately in front of you (like another car or a party of American tourists), put the car into 'D' (for Drive) and *slowly* press the accelerator. Extremely lightly will be enough. Do the same in 'R' (for Reverse). If the car is a front-wheel-drive vehicle, then during these tests the rear of the car should rise when in 'R'. If it is a rear-wheel-drive vehicle, then the front of the car should rise when in 'D'. This indicates a healthy transmission system. If the car stalls, or the engine noise fades, suspect trouble.

Having a replacement transmission system is a most expensive procedure.

Axle
There are few easy tests which you can perform here, you just have to listen for noises. There is one though — take hold of the propshaft (propellor shaft), if you can, (the tubular pole which extends from

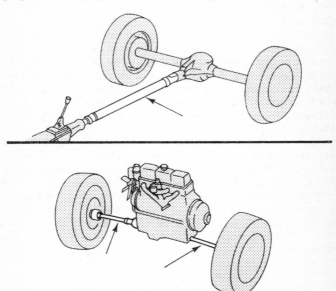

Fig. 21
Top: Rear-wheel-drive car with propshaft.
Bottom: Front-wheel-drive car with driveshafts.

the back of the gearbox to the back axle, directly down the middle of the car) when the car is in neutral, and rock it gently. It should be perfectly tight. A drone from the axle ends (near the back wheels), whilst in motion indicates worn wheel bearings (which aren't cheap to repair but not catastrophic). Noises from the middle of the axle, whilst in motion — none should be discernible — indicate a worn differential which is much more pricey to replace. If when you engage reverse and depress the accelerator, there is a clunking noise, of something engaging underneath the car, it suggests a worn propshaft which, again, can be expensive.

Many smaller cars are front-wheel-drive vehicles. They do not have propshafts, but have driveshafts where the front wheels are driven directly from the gearbox. The same 'rocking' test can be performed on each driveshaft. The driveshafts can be found quite easily — they're the short, fat tubular poles extending from the middle of each front wheel to either side of the gearbox.

Clutch

A good practical and well-known test for checking whether a clutch is in good order is to do the following: sit in the driver's seat and start the engine. Engage second gear and the handbrake. Rev the car up to above mid-way and slowly let the clutch out. If the car's revs decrease proportionately to your letting the clutch out, or the car stalls completely then, it's okay. If not, then it's slipping and is either worn or has oil on it. Either way it will need replacing shortly.

When you depress the clutch the operation should be smooth and there should be no noise. A whirring noise, when depressed indicates wear of the release bearing which will need replacing shortly. A new release bearing itself is not expensive (a few pounds only), but the gearbox will usually have to be taken off to get to it which is a time-consuming and, therefore costly process. Take the handbrake off and, on a level road, using clutch control, pull away from stationary in second gear. The car should not stall and should accelerate smoothly.

Tyres

Check the condition of all the tyres. Look for general overall wear and judge how long it will be before you need to replace them. On older cars, check if they are radials (generally fatter and have a criss-crossed tread pattern which strays up the sides of the tyres) or crossply (where the tread usually stops before going up the sides of the tyres and does not criss-cross). *Remember* that you should *never* mix radial and crossply on the *same* axle, it's very dangerous. Radials should be at the back and crossply on the front. Anyway, it is inadvisable to mix different types of tyres on the same car; they perform in completely different ways and do not complement each other. It is inadvisable even to mix different makes of tyre.

Check the wear of the tyres, whether it is even across the tread. Wear on one side suggests a wheel needs balancing, the tracking (rods, ends, bushes) need attention or, more seriously, the chassis or sub-frame is buckled, perhaps due to an encounter with a kerbside. Look for cuts, swelling, abrasions — again, the result of being damaged on a kerbside, a brick, a pothole. Check whether the tyres are all the same make which indicates a considerate no-expense-spared owner.

On a personal note, I never buy remoulds. I know that they're much cheaper than brand new tyres, but they're also much more dangerous. I have known many instances where remoulds have simply disintegrated when cars have been travelling at high speeds. If you are going to buy remoulds, then simply don't drive fast.

Is it really worth it?

This may all sound tremendously time-consuming, a dirty business and a complete pain-in-the-neck, but do remember that an uncomfortable hour or two can save you hundreds of pounds in the long run. When you look at it like that it'll almost be fun (personally, I enjoy all this stuff, but each to his own) and after a couple of times you'll get the hang of it and it'll take no time at all. Practise on your neighbours', friends' or family cars to get a good idea of what to look for and what sounds right and wrong.

The Test Drive

Providing that you are properly insured, then it is fine to test drive the car (if in doubt consult your broker). If you are not insured then don't fear, it's not absolutely necessary to test drive yourself as long as you follow the instructions in this book, observe the seller/driver carefully, and ask him to do a few things. Make sure that the driver is not avoiding problems by carefully rounding corners, braking very cautiously and the like, perhaps trying to hide a fault. Also, and this is important, make sure the radio remains switched off. There's plenty of time to check it later and you're not on a joy ride here. The sound of the radio may be covering up other noises. Make sure you open a window so that you can listen for noises outside, even if it's raining.

1. Ask the seller to start up the car but observe carefully. All cars differ as to how they like to be started (lots of choke, a little choke, put the choke in, put the choke out, do the Okeechokee, etc.) and you'll get used to it in time. If you start the car up and aren't aware of its peculiarities, you may flood the engine and give yourself a

false impression as to its condition. If the car has difficulty starting, it's not necessarily a major problem. It may just need new points or plugs (see chapter 11, page 101). However the compression may be too low (very expensive). If so, it may cough and splutter, conk out and need a few more turns of the key, connect but only slowly pick up power.

2. Start the engine and listen to the sound the engine makes. There should be an even running with no noises (grinding, spluttering, coughing, whirring or knocking). It takes years of practice to be able to say which noise means what (like a doctor and your symptoms) but remember that any noise means trouble, and as a general rule the worse the noise the worse the trouble. Do make sure you allow the car to warm up a little though. Even new cars don't like running cold.

3. Once the car is warmed up fully, make sure that the road is clear, put your foot down and see how much power (acceleration) the car has. There should be no juddering, no spluttering and quite a bit of power (there are only two people in a car designed to take twice the load and luggage). But don't expect a Ferrari's acceleration from a cheap bottom-of-the-range model.

4. Listen for any unhappy noise when accelerating and decelerating at all times during the test drive.

5. If the car jumps out of gear, especially when pulling up a hill, then the gearbox needs attention. It could mean the replacement of the whole box, just the selector mechanism or a small ball bearing or spring. Unfortunately the problem cannot be discovered without dismantling the entire thing. If you can't find a hill to test this out on, try leaving it until the last second (high revs) to change up a gear.

6. Make sure you stop the car, and using clutch control start moving the car in second gear. Although a car is not designed to do this, if the engine is in good condition it should, easily and smoothly, with no knocking sounds, jerkiness or stalling.

7. Find a hill. Stop the car before you get to the top and test the handbrake. Try a hill start, which the car should perform without any difficulty. When over the crown take your foot off the accelerator, leave it in gear and let the car roll down the other side of its own volition. When nearing the bottom put your foot down to the floor and

accelerate away (if it's safe to do so). Look through the rear view mirror and check if the car sends out a trail of smoke. It may give off a little smoke, due to the build up of unused oil, but not an excessive amount, which would indicate engine wear.

8. Whilst test driving make sure, again when it's very safe to do so (preferably in the country), that you brake with your hands placed only very gently on the wheel (do this only when going very slowly). Don't brake too harshly but just enough to make sure the car maintains a steady line straight ahead. If it pulls to one side, it may be due to something as simple as one tyre which is under-inflated, but there are also plenty of other reasons why this may happen, requiring thorough brakes' inspection and overhaul. It could also suggest a bent chassis, through accidental damage, and that will require further inspection. If the car constantly pulls to one side when driving, then the tracking may be out of alignment.

9. If the car should vibrate during the test drive, or you feel considerable vibration through the steering wheel (usually at a higher speed) the wheels may need balancing (a cheap process).

10. Particularly listen for clunks and bangs when going round corners, which may indicate either steering, suspension or shock absorbers wear. Make sure first that there are no items rolling about in the boot which may give you a false impression.

11. Before you turn off the engine at the end of the test drive, check that the temperature gauge is at the 'normal' position, or in the middle of the dial. It should not be either too hot or too cold, or there may be a cooling system problem (blown head gasket, water leak, blocked radiator matrix or pipe, air lock, etc.). Observe that the oil pressure gauge (if fitted) reads between a quarter and half way up the scale at tickover and normal operating temperature. Also note that the gauge should fall back to zero when the engine is switched off. Don't consider this or any of the gauges in the car to be the final word on the subject. Gauges, especially those in older cars, aren't made that well, or to last. If the engine is running too hot there should be a smell of "burning" rubber from the engine, which may permeate through to the interior.

Assessment
More often than not with a used car you will find one or more, or even many faults. A small fault here and there may be more an advantage

than a disadvantage. You may be able to negotiate a discount for repairs in excess of the money it will actually cost you. *Look* for faults, make sure you find a fault. It may only be a minor one but by bringing it to the attention of the seller you may well get him to make a price reduction, certainly enough to fix the problem. If you inspect a car fully and come up with no problems at all, and even praise the car, the seller may think he is underselling the vehicle and might not be prepared to haggle.

Also, by finding faults, you allow yourself a get-out clause from striking the deal there and then. You can say, that before discussing the deal you have to check out how much it will cost to have the repairs made. This will allow you time perhaps to pop down the local garage and question a mechanic as to what a particular noise coming from a particular part of the car means, and cost-up any repairs.

You will do yourself a favour by buying time, time to think and be objective. If you have some problem or other with the car, or you simply don't feel comfortable about the seller, then say that you need to think about it over night and you will let them know. Of course they may say that there are a number of other interested people coming to view the car between now and then, and it may be sold. Say "Okay, if it's sold, it's sold". Don't be pressured into taking a wrong decision.

Do remember that if a car hasn't rotted through to the chassis everything *can* be fixed and/or replaced. It's up to you to judge whether the problems are worth the lowest price the seller is prepared to accept. Simply cost-up the repairs and take them off the price you think is fair. Do also remember that there are thousands of cars each week to choose from and you shouldn't rush into a purchase just because it's raining and you can't be bothered to tramp around any more.

Having said all that though, make sure that you don't let a real bargain slip through your fingers, by being over-cautious or too suspicious, or by over-deliberating. Be confident and know what you want. Use this book to help you recognise a bargain when you see one and don't let anyone else pip you to the post. However, there is undoubtedly more than one bargain available from week to week; indeed there may be lots.

I don't want to confuse you but, as I've already said, buying a used car is *not* an exact science. It's all a question of balance and weighing up the pros and cons of any individual situation.

A good tip, which may help you in your decision, is to make a note of the last owner (as detailed on the registration document), if you're dealing with someone who hasn't owned the car long or a trader. While you're thinking about it, over night, call them and ask them about the car. They'll know more about the car than anyone else. They will no doubt be honest, as they will have got their money and have no more interest in the car and, therefore, no reason to mislead you. Ask them why they sold it? Does it have any faults? Say that whilst you respect the seller, or the dealer, you simply want a second opinion. Run through your list of twenty questions again (on page 22), especially the one about the mileage.

Documentation Inspection

The next step is carefully to inspect the car's documentation. 'Inspect' does not mean a cursory glance to see that it's all there, it means a detailed and thorough going-over.

MOT (DEPARTMENT OF TRANSPORT TEST) CERTIFICATE:

1. Check that the registration number tallies with that shown on the MOT document and in turn that it corresponds with the registration plates on the car (front and back).

2. Check that the mileage when last tested corresponds to that displayed on the mileometer in the car (bearing in mind a reasonable additional mileage since that date).

3. Check when the certificate runs out and when the car will have to be submitted for its next yearly inspection.

4. Check that the cubic capacity (cc) of the engine corresponds with that shown on the registration document.

5. Check that the certificate has been stamped (usually with an impress machine) at the bottom right-hand corner with the name and address of the testing station.

6. Check that the year of manufacture corresponds with that shown on the registration document.

REGISTRATION DOCUMENT

1. Check that the name and address of the seller is that shown in the box, top left-hand corner. Check the previous owner (if any) who is also detailed and hope that it doesn't say 'Police', 'Park Rangers' or the like.

2. Check the registration number shown is the same as the plates on the car.

3. Check the taxation class, usually 'private/light goods'.

4. Check the make and the model (that it really is an L, GL, GTi or coupé, etc.).

5. Check the colour and that the car has not been resprayed. The colour will normally be a simple basic colour such as red, green, blue, black, white, etc., and not in glorious advertising or manufacturerspeak such as Waterloo Crimson, Pacific Island Azure, Anthracite Welsh Valley Very Very Shiny Black, Virgin Diamond Arctic Bear White-as-the-Polar-Cap White.

6. Check that the engine and body numbers correspond to those shown on the car.

7. Check the date of registration, whether it is a 1986 C reg or a 1985 C reg.

8. Check how many keepers it has had and when the last change of keeper took place.

SERVICE HISTORY
These are the documents which show how well the car has been looked after. If there are no documents available then you have no idea whether it has been regularly serviced or not, and will have to rely on your impression from your inspection. It may have only bills for parts or work that has been done, which is better than nothing. It may, however, come with a complete and full service history where the car has been serviced after every 6,000, 10,000 or 12,000 miles. The garage will have stamped the Service book when work took place and you will have an accurate record. Watch that this document has not been forged. It should be perhaps a little tatty and worn and the stamps may be different colours, have faded slightly and been initialled or signed with pens of different coloured inks.

Professional Inspection
The AA and RAC offer a vehicle inspection service, where you pay them a sum of money and they will come round and check out a vehicle fully and give you a comprehensive and authoritative report. It's a very good service and you'll really know the pros and cons of the vehicle before you buy it. It has its drawbacks though, as it can take a while to set up this inspection, by which time the car may have been

sold. It is also pricey, and if you're checking out a number of cars the total cost can become exorbitant. What I suggest is that you contact a local garage, perhaps where you have done business before or who someone recommends, and ask them if they provide this service. Most of them will and the inspection may well be as comprehensive. It's likely to be much cheaper and possibly you'll be able to arrange it in advance, so you won't gamble on losing the car. But first and foremost check out the car for yourself, using this book.

9

DIRTY TRICKS TO LOOK OUT FOR

Let it first be said that the majority of used car motor dealers and private individuals are an honest bunch. This may be contrary to popular belief but it is the truth. Not everyone is a con artist. This may contradict the opinion of some friends and relatives, but do remember that you only hear stories about bad car deals, not good ones, because misfortune is entertaining (human beings take great pleasure from the mistakes made by others). However, there *are* dodgy dealers nationwide, and although a private individual may be the most honest person in the world under normal circumstances, when it comes to selling an old motor everyone can be, shall we say, economical with the truth. So it is wise to be aware of the dirty tricks that can be played.

When a car develops a fault, whatever it may be, it normally lets you know about it well in advance. A rattle here, a crack there, a whistle, a knocking, a bang. A fuse may blow but a mechanical part doesn't very often just 'go'. It goes slowly, over time. Mechanical parts wear out and have to be replaced (if you want to know the scientific reason why this is, take a night class). A fanbelt can snap at any time with no warning and all parts of any machine have a limited life expectancy; but as a general rule, as parts wear out, they wear *down*. As they do, so gaps are created in the working mechanism and in these spaces vibrations begin and noises are the result.

A noise indicates a fault. A noisy car is difficult to sell because everyone knows that from babies to washing machines, from water cisterns to hip joints, noises indicate trouble. To stop a noise you have to fix a fault and that can be expensive. *You can,* however, stop it for a short period of time, at least until the car has been sold.

There follows a list of various tricks and cons which I have, over the years, encountered. Look out for them. I've saved myself and other people a fortune by being able to spot them a mile off.

1. Cataloy Paste, plastic padding or bodyfiller is available in any high street car-part shop or supermarket. Anyone who has owned an older car will have found a use for this remarkable substance, for filling in the holes created by the effects of rust. If done properly, and then sprayed over, it is very difficult to find where this substance has been applied (even after careful eye and finger inspection). There's nothing wrong with it if used properly. All cars rust and need constant renovation.

But the problem with filler is that most people do not use it properly or in the right places. They very rarely follow the instructions on the can. They take short-cuts. For example, not all the rust is removed, filler is applied on a wet or dirty surface, or rust preventer is not used. In these cases, rust redevelops very quickly and the job needs doing again. This is particularly true of people wishing to sell their car. They do not care whether or not it lasts. It's certainly not going to rust after a week or so, so why bother doing a really good job? But if they show a car with a hole, it's going to put an awful lot of people off. It is therefore important to be able to check whether filler has been applied to a car. How to tell:

a) Look along the bodywork with your ear on the panel. You will then be able to see whether there is any irregularity in the contours of the surface. If the filler has not been 'rubbed down' properly (sand papered smooth) it will show either above or below the surface.

b) Feel along the surface for any roughness.

c) It is sometimes difficult after 'filling' a car to paint over it well. Touch-up paint is not easy to apply and it is not easy to get the right sheen. Check that the texture of the paint is even all over each panel.

d) The easiest way to check for filler is by the use of a magnet. Filler has no metal in it. A magnet will not adhere to a car's body where a quantity of filler exists underneath. So take a magnet with you and run it over the body. This method does not work on aluminium or fibre glass cars or areas where filler has been only lightly applied, skimmed. Make sure that the magnet is wrapped in an old handkerchief to avoid scratching the paintwork.

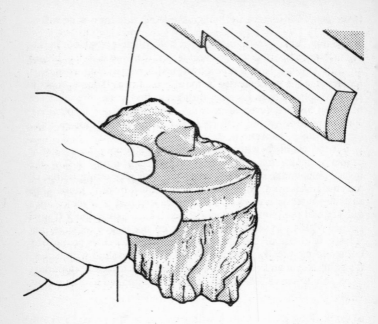

Fig. 22 Running a magnet over the body.

2. The interior look of a car is very important to a prospective purchaser, a fact recognised by dealers and private sellers alike. Indeed, to some foolish people, the look of a car is often much more important than the condition of the engine or the structure. People fall in love with cars on first sight. Dealers use a substance known as 'lacquer' to buff-up the look of the interior of a car, particularly the dashboard and seats. Lacquer can make anything that it is applied to (by spray) look brand new — for a short period of time only. Beware a sparkling interior and a tell-tale smell of drying paint (its characteristic aroma). This is not really a 'dirty' trick but it's a mild form of deception nonetheless.

3. "Clocking", the common term for turning back the mileage on a car (showing that the car has done fewer miles than it actually has), is illegal and widespread. Be wary of a dealer who won't guarantee the mileage (he may suspect that it has been "clocked",

if he hasn't done it himself). Look for telltale signs as described on page 73. Dealers have been known to pick up high mileage, ex-company and fleet cars at auctions and turn back the clocks. Regard any ex-company vehicle with a low average yearly mileage with suspicion. A dealer may try to fob you off with statements such as "the cable has snapped", "the dashboard has been swapped" or "it *might* have a reconditioned engine".

4. Be wary if, when you arrive to view a car, it is spotless and shiny, the windows sparkle and the paintwork glistens. All you have to be cautious of here is *yourself.* It's not a crime for someone to polish up a car for sale − it's perfectly understandable, as everyone wants whatever they're selling to appear in its best possible light. *You,* however, may be taken in by appearances. How many times have you been attracted to someone simply because of the way they look, only to be disappointed later when they turn out to be as thick as two short planks? Particularly beware of highly polished glass. A great percentage of any vehicle is comprised of glass which is probably the most durable part of a car. A rusty old heap can be made fairly presentable if the glasswork is prepared properly. So, just be careful, and as a general rule don't be taken in by appearances (the car or the seller).

5. Some rather unscrupulous individuals have been known to mix woodshavings or sawdust in the gearbox. This, unsurprisingly, wrecks the gearbox mechanism after a short time. Immediately, however, it has the effect of keeping an old and tired box from dying an imminent death, at least until a prospective purchaser has paid for the car and driven it home. Unfortunately, it is not always easy to check, when inspecting a car before purchase, whether internal items such as the gearbox are excessively worn or have been illegitimately tampered with. Look for telltale signs of sawdust and the like, which may have been scattered over the box and collected in the casing dirt. This practice is, fortunately, no longer in fashion and it is unlikely that you will come across it.

6. Be suspicious of a car that is locked when on a forecourt or at an auction, when the others are left open for inspection. The seller may not want the interior to be inspected. Also beware if you are unable, or indeed are discouraged (for whatever reason), from looking under the bonnet or the boot. Yes, there may be a perfectly credible reason for this, after all release cables have been known

to snap, but another far more suspect reason is that an inspection could reveal inner-panel rot or some other serious problem. If a private seller won't show you the engine, then simply walk away.

7. Double-check on the registration document that the information given corresponds with the badges which the car displays — eg 1600cc, 2 litre, GTi, L, GL, S. It is not illegal to drive around in a 1300 which displays a 1800GL badge. It *is* illegal to sell any item as one thing when it really is something else — that's misrepresentation.

8. By retarding the engine timing it is possible to disguise the fact that the big end is on the way out. Question any car which does not rev easily, especially at high revs.

9. If you hear a metallic rattle coming from the top of the engine block, it may be due to worn tappets. The seller may tell you that this indeed is merely the tappets rattling, and they simply need adjusting. It could be nothing really to concern yourself about, as tappets wear loose and require tightening occasionally. It could, however, be that they have been tightened as far as they will go and are so worn that they still rattle. This is serious and can be expensive as they will need replacing. Over-tightening the tappets causes a loss in performance and can be discovered during a test drive. Put your foot down and see if the car accelerates effectively.

10. Always have a cursory glance at the brake, clutch and accelerator pedals in the cabin. The rubber on these pedals wears down with use. If a car displays only 20,000 miles and the rubbers are worn down to the metal, then suspect that the car may have been "clocked". If the rubbers are new then suspect that they have been replaced and the car has been "clocked". Ask why they were replaced. It's not easy to judge precisely what amount of wear represents what amount of mileage — that's quite an expert job. But you can use this information in a general overall assessment of the kind of life a car has led.

11. Make sure that glued-down carpets, in the boot and in the cabin, are not hiding rust holes.

12. Always check that the gearstick goes into all the gears displayed

on the gearknob. It is not unknown for four-speed cars to display five-speed gearknobs.

13. Always look under the bonnet for loose wires, particularly ones that have been deliberately cut rather than worn (shiny ended and not corroded). They could be the connection from the oil warning light or engine temperature gauge which, if connected, might disclose a serious fault.

14. Oil additives (such as STP, PTFE) added to an engine serve to aid lubrication of the moving parts and help to reduce wear (particularly useful in older and performance car engines). It doesn't stop wear, however, and parts eventually wear out due to use. When these parts wear out they often begin to make strange noises which are tell-tale signs of a tired engine. The manufacturers generally recommend one can of such additive for each oil change.

The excessive use of such substances (five or six cans, for example), can hide engine noises for a short time. Of course that doesn't mean that the faults will go away, it just covers them up temporarily.

15. Make sure that you place your hand on the bonnet of the car as one of the first tests you make. Why? To check whether the engine is warm or not. (If the car is a rear engined vehicle, then you're completely wasting your time; walk around the back and place your hand on the boot instead!). Sometimes you will have to lift the bonnet as some cars have thick insulating and sound-deadening felt underneath.

The reason for doing this is that the car may not perform well when cold, the automatic choke may not work, the timing may be dodgy, but when warm these faults disappear. Watch for people who arrange exact times for you to view the car — it may have been recently driven. They might be trying to cover up something. They may, of course, just have driven their invalid mother down to the shops, so don't be too critical. Just take it into consideration when weighing up all the facts.

16. At an auction beware specifically of the following:

a) As mentioned on page 91, a car with locked doors when all the other cars' doors are open. The owner may not want you to perform the usual interior tests, or press a spongy clutch or brake pedal, or want you to open up the engine compartment for an inspection.

b) Occasionally a prospective purchaser (usually a dealer), who has already checked the car out, seen it drive in to the auction okay and given it a clean bill of health, may switch the spark plug leads around. This will cause the car to fire erratically and put off the competition. This is not easy to detect if you are not an expert but do watch anyone pawing over the engine of a car you are interested in. Make your presence felt.

c) For the same reason, people have been known to put honey or sugar in the petrol tank of a car which, in small amounts, doesn't harm the engine very much, but does produce a lovely lot of black smoke from the exhaust which can be very off-putting.

d) The windscreen ticket provided by the auctioneer with information about the car on it should be permanently displayed. Be wary of a car that doesn't have such a ticket until the last minute. The owner may want you to overlook some detail, such as the car having been written-off, used as a taxi (described as a Hackney Carriage), having unwarranted mileage, being sold 'as seen' or having no MOT.

e) Watch out for the owner who insists on starting up the car himself (rather than the auction driver), or insists on accompanying the driver into the ring. He could be there to tell the driver that something doesn't work properly and show him how to overcome the problem.

10

YOUR CAR AND THE LAW

Road Tax

Any vehicle which is kept, parked or used on the road, whether it works or not, must display a valid tax disc (applicable to that car only). The *only* two exceptions to this rule are (a) when driving to and from an appointed MOT test, or (b) during the fourteen days grace period allowed after the expiry date of the last tax disc (provided that a replacement has been applied for in advance and you continue to display the old disc) — a little scribbled note saying "tax in the post" or "tax applied for" is no use whatsoever and doesn't fool anyone.

Road tax can be obtained at any major post office. In order to purchase a tax disc you will have to provide evidence of insurance covering you for that car, a valid MOT certificate (if applicable, i.e. if it is over three years old) and proof of ownership (registration document with your name and address on it), a completed form and requisite fee. It is an offence to drive an un-taxed car or not to display the tax disc (whether you have one or not, or it has been stolen or simply has fallen off the windscreen). If you lose your tax disc, or it is stolen, a replacement can be obtained by completing a form V20. If you surrender a disc in advance of its expiry date you can obtain a refund. Normally a private car will still have some tax left when you buy it, whereas with a dealer or auction car you will usually need to tax it yourself. Do so before you drive it. You will not be able to tax your car without evidence of insurance. Therefore be sure to call your insurance company, or agent and arrange to have a cover note or certificate ready to hand.

MOT Certificate

After a car has been registered for three years/is three years old it requires a valid MOT (Ministry of Transport) Test Certificate of roadworthiness. This comprehensive test covers such aspects as the effectiveness of seat belts (not whether they are fitted but whether they work), exhaust emissions and general condition, indicators, brakes, wheel bearings, lights, windscreen wipers and wiper blades, screen washers, speedometer efficiency, ball joints, trackrods, tyre tread and condition, steering, dashboard warning lights, body condition and suspension. If you were to have an accident and your car was not MOT'd, your insurance company might well call on you personally to repay any claim arising.

Insurance in the U.K.
It is the law that all motorists must be insured against public liability, because it is presumed that most people would not be able to pay damages awarded against them for serious public injury. This is fair and ensures that any injured party can receive damages caused through a motorist's negligence.

The law requires no more than Third Party Insurance, that is, against injury to other people. However, most policies wisely include cover against damage to property and possessions.

If a car cannot be moved (even if parked on the road) or is parked on private land then there is no need to insure it. If it can be moved, whether you intend to move it or not, you must be insured for that vehicle. Motor Insurance covers a person (and other nominated drivers) and not a vehicle (or vehicles), although it is usual to have to specify which vehicle or vehicles you require the insurance for (whether owned by you or not).

Insurance costs vary depending on such factors as what kind of car you intend driving, how old you are, how long you have been a driver, whether you have any motoring convictions (or penalty points), where you live, the purpose you use the vehicle for (business or pleasure or both), whether it is garaged or not, whether you have any no claims bonus and your occupation. Costs are generally calculated by estimating any potential claim made after an accident and, considering all the factors, how likely you are to have an accident. If you lie about *any* information asked of you by your insurers, or indeed do not divulge any information relevant to the policy (even if you're not asked for it), they are at liberty to refuse to pay any compensation charges. You must act in good faith and be 100% accurate. Remember, ignorance is no excuse in the eyes of the law, so be informed and inform your insurers. If you are considering misleading your insurers, by lying about your occupation, where you live or the power of your car in order to avoid paying the full amount, then forget it — you may as well not be insured at all. *Important:* Insure yourself properly at all times.

Legal history is full of examples whereby individuals thought that they were fully insured when, in fact, their insurers were at liberty to refuse to pay out in the event of a claim. It is therefore worth considering a few of the most common mistakes that are made, as the law tends to favour insurance companies. In general, companies will not be unreasonable, but it is foolish to rely on their good nature.

1. Tell your insurers if you have had insurance refused in the past, for any reason.

2. Inform your insurers of all the details of all the people who will be driving under your policy.

3. Don't suffer from ignorance, make sure that all those insured under your policy (the named drivers) do not have any convictions themselves.

4. Be specific as to what your occupation really is, don't embroider the truth.

5. Read the small print contained within the policy. A lot of people don't bother.

6. Don't use the car for business purposes when it is only insured for domestic and pleasure purposes.

7. Don't carry more passengers than your car is designed for (i.e. do not overload).

8. Make sure your tyres have the legal amount of tread.

9. Make sure all your lights work, perform a weekly check.

10. Regularly service the car. If an accident is caused through, say, defective brakes your insurers may refuse to pay on the grounds that the vehicle was not maintained properly.

11. Report any accident you may have to your insurance company whether there was a claim made or not.

Important: shop around for insurance, take the advice of friends in this matter. There are good insurance companies and there are bad. There are companies who will pay out in the event of a legitimate claim, promptly and without any fuss, there are others who will hassle you, delay indefinitely and refuse to pay when you

are entitled to compensation. As a general rule, it is wise to be
prepared to pay a little bit more for insurance through a reputable
company, or on the recommendation of a reputable agent, simply
because it is so important. I sincerely hope that you enjoy an
accident-free motoring life, but it is very likely that you will have
an accident of some form at one time or another and it is best to
be confident in the company backing you.

Registration Document

This is the computerised successor to what used to be called a 'log
book', and some people call it a 'log book' still. It details the
registered keeper of any particular vehicle (not necessarily the
owner), the engine and body numbers, the number of previous
keepers (and the last one's address), its colour, the engine's cubic
capacity (cc), the taxation class, the vehicle's date of registration,
the registration number and its seating capacity. This document tells
you a great deal about a vehicle. It is not proof that the seller owns
the car but make sure always to check that the name and address
of the seller is that which is displayed on the registration document.
When a vehicle is sold, both parties, buyer and seller, must notify
the DVLC *immediately*. The seller does so by completing and
sending the tear-off bottom part of the document, and the buyer
by completing and sending the rest, the main part.

A new registration document, in the buyer's name, usually arrives
by post approximately one month after being sent, but it may take
longer. Lost registration documents can be replaced by completing
a form V62 which is available at any major post office. Not many
people know this, but you can obtain a full list of *all* previous owners
of the vehicle by writing to the DVLC. All these services are free
of charge.

Vehicle Maintenance

It is a common fault to believe that your duty to maintain a safe
and roadworthy vehicle is limited to the yearly MOT test. Both the
owner and the driver can be prosecuted for any breach of
regulations, as set out in The Motor Vehicle (Conditions of Use)
Regulations which contain 146 provisions and 11 schedules. Please
don't bother to read it; it is one of the most boring publications
I have ever read. You could, of course, amaze your friends with
such tantalising questions as "did you know that indicators must
flash between 60 and 120 times per minute?" but you'd probably
never be invited to a party again! You can be convicted of an offence

against these Regulations even if you were unaware that you were in breach. Most of the conditions though, are common sense, and an offence such as a blown light bulb would not stand you a king's ransom in court, if you were ever taken there for such an offence (which is highly unlikely). Very briefly, they run as follows — more details at the back of the Highway Code:-

MIRRORS: you must have a rear view mirror but wing mirrors are not necessary for private cars. Commercial vehicles need door/wing mirrors but not necessarily an inside one.

BRAKES: the handbrake and footbrake operating all four wheels must be effective and capable of stopping a car at a reasonable distance (see Highway Code).

SILENCER: to be effective.

HORN: mustn't be used unnecessarily (e.g. for attracting the attention of a friend in a shop) or at night (unless in a dire emergency). Bells, sirens and two-tones are not allowed. The horn must work.

LIGHTS: they all must work and be kept clean (often forgotten, especially in bad weather). There should be no red lights at the front. There should be no white lights at the back (other than reversing light(s) which should only operate when reverse gear is engaged).

PARKING: at least 15 metres away from any junction.

SPEEDOMETER: must be accurate to 10% at anything over 10 miles per hour.

WINDSCREEN WIPERS: are compulsory and must work effectively.

SEAT BELTS: the wearing of them is compulsory in the front of a car and has been since 1983. Cars made before it was compulsory for manufacturers to fit them (1963) don't need to have them and some commercial vehicles (taxis, etc.) are also exempt. If belts are fitted in the rear of the car, then children travelling in the back must be secured at all times.

The Law and Buying a Used Car
A car is a consumer item and is thus subject to the consumer laws.

Many used cars are bought and sold by private individuals and the purchaser will not be protected by the Sale of Goods Act, but you will be if buying from a dealer.

If repair work is carried out by members of the Motor Agents' Association (MAA) or the Society of Motor Manufacturers and Traders (SMMT) then they are expected to abide by a Code of Practice, which sets standards which are to be maintained. If you feel that the Code has been broken, then you can apply for arbitration. Even if the garage is not a member of one of these organisations you could be covered, when suing in a county court, because the Code shows standards expected of any 'reasonable' garage.

11

WHAT TO DO IF THE CAR WON'T START

If a car will not start, don't immediately consider it useless. It could be something very simple and cheap to fix. Check the following:

1. If the engine will only turn over very slowly, not enough to fire, check the battery terminals for tightness and for corrosion. They may not be allowing enough charge to pass to the starter motor. If you clean them carefully (with a wire brush and sandpaper) and if the problem still exists after you make sure they are tightened up properly, then suspect a poorly charged battery. There may be an alternator fault or a worn-out battery. Try a jump-lead start. If *that* will not turn the engine over vigorously, it's probably a worn starter motor which will need replacing.

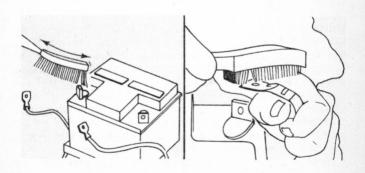

Fig. 23 Cleaning the battery terminals.

2. If the car will not start but the engine turns over energetically, check for a spark at the plugs. Take out one plug, re-attach its lead

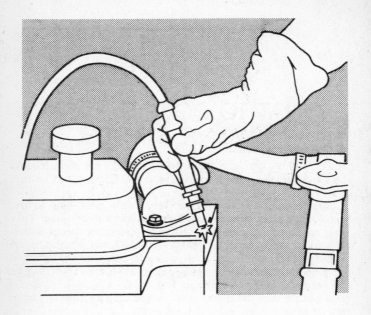

Fig. 24 Looking for a spark.

and lie it, or hold it (using an insulator to avoid a shock), with the
fat metal part touching the engine block (the part from which you
removed the plug) and turn the engine over. (You may find it just
as easy to hold the outer electrode touching the engine block, as
in fig. 24.) Keep hands, clothing, etc., clear of moving parts. There
should be a cracking good spark at the tip of the plug. (If you do
not have a plug spanner handy, then roll up a piece of silver paper
(perhaps from a cigarette packet), shove it in the plug insulator cap
and see if a spark will jump a ½mm gap to the block instead. Again,
insulate your hands and stay clear of moving items.)

   If there is a spark, then smell the hole where the spark plug came
from. If the car has been turned over a few times, it should reek
of petrol. If there is no smell of petrol, then suspect an empty tank.
Check this by rocking the car at the rear and listening for any moving
liquid (never trust the petrol gauge). If there is petrol there, suspect
a fuel pump, fuel line or carburettor problem.

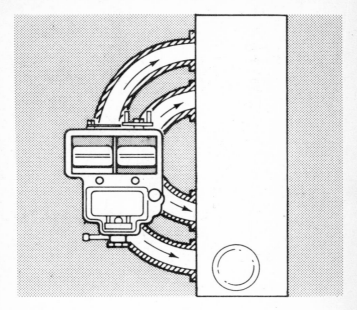

Fig. 25   The carburettor (with the air filter removed).

3. There's not much you can do about a fuel pump or line problem on a quick inspection. Check the carburettor though by taking off the air filter (which usually covers it and is quite easy to remove) and look inside the filter for a blockage. The car may start with the air filter off, proving it needs a clean or renewal. Look at the carburettor and see if the inlet is wet with petrol (if not, then the problem is with the pump or the line). If it is wet, then check that the slide (or butterfly valve) which regulates the mixture of petrol and air is not stuck. It may be possible to free it using oil. *No* smoking or sparks while this test is done.

4. If there isn't a spark, take off the distributor cap, turn the engine over (or rather have someone turn the car engine for you) and look for a spark at the points. If there is no spark, then it's possibly points failure. You can test this by leaving the ignition switched on and, using a screwdriver or pencil, opening and closing the points. A spark should be released. If there still isn't a spark, then it's probably

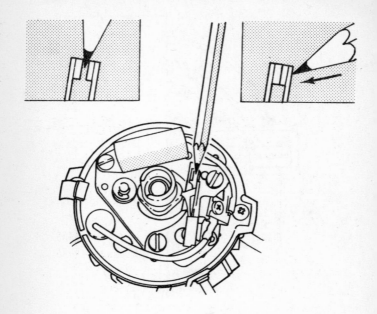

Fig. 26 Open and close the points.

a coil or condenser problem and one of them will need replacing.

5. If there is a smell of petrol and a spark at the plugs, then the engine is probably flooded (too much petrol because of too much choke). Put the choke in (if automatic choke then it could be faulty) and try the car again a few times with the accelerator pressed down. If it soon begins to fire, you will have found the cause.

6. If the weather is particularly humid or wet, then it could simply be damp in the engine. Use a cloth to dry off any obvious damp and then a can of water repellent (a damp starting spray or WD40) and spray liberally over the fuses, the battery terminals, the coil and condenser, the plug leads, inside and out of the distributor. Leave a short while and try to start the car again.

12

REGISTRATION NUMBERS

No prefix or suffix pre-February 1963

Suffix Letters

A	February 1963 to December 1963
B	January 1964 to December 1964
C	January 1965 to December 1965
D	January 1966 to December 1966
E	January 1967 to July 1967
F	August 1967 to July 1968
G	August 1968 to July 1969
H	August 1969 to July 1970
J	August 1970 to July 1971
K	August 1971 to July 1972
L	August 1972 to July 1973
M	August 1973 to July 1974
N	August 1974 to July 1975
P	August 1975 to July 1976
R	August 1976 to July 1977
S	August 1977 to July 1978
T	August 1978 to July 1979
V	August 1979 to July 1980
W	August 1980 to July 1981
X	August 1981 to July 1982
Y	August 1982 to July 1983

Prefix Letters

A	August 1983 to July 1984
B	August 1984 to July 1985
C	August 1985 to July 1986
D	August 1986 to July 1987
E	August 1987 to July 1988
F	August 1988 to July 1989
G	August 1989 to July 1990
H	August 1990 to July 1991

Imported vehicles used to be allocated suffix letters to indicate the date when they were brought into the country. Since 1983 they have been allocated letters to determine the first year when they were used, either in the UK or abroad. Nowadays, the letter Q is used for kit cars, cars made up of various bits of other cars, cars where the year of manufacture cannot be determined and those which do not have surviving documentation or record. If in doubt, always consult the registration document (if available) which should detail when the car was first used and first registered in the UK. To determine the origin of a particular vehicle, consult your local vehicle tax office. Vehicles registered in Jersey are prefixed by a 'J', in Guernsey they contain no letters, just numbers. In the Isle of Man they include the letters 'MAN' and in Ireland they have an 'I' or a 'Z' in their combinations.

13

ADVERTISING SHORTHAND

(in alphabetical order)

There follows a list of abbreviations commonly used, for the sake of economy, to describe cars advertised for sale in newspapers and magazines, car windscreens, etc.

A or Alloys	Alloy Wheels
A or Auto	Automatic Transmission
ABS	Anti-lock Braking System
a/c	Air conditioning
BHP	Brake Horse Power
c/locking or C/L	Central Locking
concours	Showroom condition
DHC	Drop Head Coupé
e/a	Electric Aerial
e/m or EDM	Electric Mirrors
ESR or e/s	Electric Sunroof
e/w	Electric Windows
f/f s/r	Factory fitted sunroof
FHC	Fixed Head Coupé
FSH	Full Service History
FS/RS	Front Spoiler/Rear Spoiler
HRW	Heated Rear Window
i or inj or in	Fuel Injection
LHD	Left Hand Drive
LPT or profiles	Low Profile Tyres
LSD	Limited Slip Differential
LWB	Long Wheel Base
M or Met	Metallic Paint
MFs	Mudflaps
MSR	Manual Sunroof
o/d	Overdrive
ono	Or nearest offer

PAB	Power Assisted Brakes
PAS	Power Assisted Steering
POA	Price on application
PX	Part Exchange
R/C	Radio Cassette
RHD	Right Hand Drive
RHR	Rear Head Restraints
rm	Recorded Mileage
s/r	Sunroof
SS Exhaust	Stainless Steel Exhaust
T and T	Road Taxed and MOT Tested
T or (T)	Trade (usually at end of Advert)
TG or Tints	Tinted Glass
vgc	Very good condition
w/w	Washer Wiper/Wide Wheels/Wire Wheels
wwt	White-wall tyres

14

HOW TO COMPLAIN

If you have a complaint to make about a car which you have purchased from a private individual then do not feel awkward about calling him up, or calling round, and talking to him about it, especially if something has gone wrong with a part which he said was okay. He may be prepared to offer you financial compensation to some degree or a fair refund. If he is obdurate and standoffish then you might have to resort to private legal action, and this is where the advert (which you will have retained) and the notes made of what the seller said will be invaluable. Call your local Citizens Advice Bureau and talk to them about it (their number's in the Yellow Pages). Tell them all the facts and ask their advice on the matter — it's free. Perhaps you might wish to consult your family solicitor whom you can instruct to write a letter.

If you have no luck with these approaches, you can arrange a hearing in a county court. This doesn't come cheap though, and if you lose the case then you will be liable for all the court and solicitors' expenses.

You may be able to qualify for legal aid. Again, ask your local Citizens Advice Bureau for local solicitors who operate the scheme, arrange an appointment with one of them and ask their free advice (or a nominal charge) as to whether to pursue the matter. You have fewer legal rights than you would have with a dealer (as you are not protected by the Sale of Goods Act) but if the seller has misrepresented the sale in any way, you could have a case. It's not as clear-cut in law as it should be though, and you may have to take some professional advice. Don't be put off from doing so — it could save you a lot of money.

If you have a problem with a car purchased from dealers, whether they work from an office, from home or from a garage, the problem may come under a dealer's warranty, in which case you should be okay. Talk to the salesperson whom you dealt with and if you're not happy with him, talk to his immediate superior. If you're still not satisfied then go to the top, the manager or managing director. If they are not forthcoming then you may have to consider another course of action. With dealers, the law is much more on your side.

I suggest you contact, the Citizens Advice Bureau for advice, a solicitor, and also approach the organisations in the Appendix who will look into the matter for you and arbitrate and conciliate on your behalf. If you do have a problem with a dealer they are likely to negotiate a settlement for you, as they do not want adverse publicity or bad word-of-mouth reports.

For complaints about used cars, repairs and servicing in England, Wales and Northern Ireland contact your nearest branch of the Motor Agents Association:

Motor Agents Association Ltd (Head Office)
201 Great Portland Street
London W1N 6AB
Telephone: 071 580 9122
York: 0904 638966   Baldock: 0462 95858
Bristol: 0272 293 232   Horsham: 0403 51454
Rugby: 0788 76465   Chester: 0244 347484

For complaints about car body repairs contact:
The Vehicle Builders and Repairers Association
Belmont House
Gildersome
Leeds LS27 7TW
Telephone: 0532 538333

For complaints about used cars, repairs and servicing in Scotland contact:
Scottish Motor Trade Association Ltd
3 Palmerston Place
Edinburgh EH12 5AQ
Telephone: 031 225 3643

For complaints about cars still under a manufacturer's warranty contact:
Society of Motor Manufacturers and Traders
Forbes House
Halkin Street
London SW1X 7DS
Telephone: 071 235 7000

For complaints concerning Motor Auctions contact:
The Society of Motor Auctions (SMA)
PO Box 13
Wilmslow PDO
Cheshire SK9 1LL
Telephone: 0625 536937

15

NOTES ON SPECIFIC CARS

There follow some general notes on many different makes and types of car, one of which you may be considering purchasing. Just because a car *looks* good and you're told by the manufacturer and the advertising people that it *is* the best thing since sliced bread, doesn't mean to say that it's any good at all. It's their job to sell cars, to glossily highlight their good points and forget altogether their shortcomings. The car could, quite possibly, be a load of rubbish; it could be made badly, it could rust to pieces after six months, it could have serious and numerous design flaws, it could be uncomfortable and difficult to drive or difficult to see out of.

You have a tremendous advantage over the person buying a new car since your prospective purchase has probably been around a while by now. The design faults may have been rectified from year to year and you have expert, unbiased and objective reports to base your judgement on. The best source of information I have found (other than someone who has owned such a car and therefore has first-hand experience which they may be willing to pass on) is the 'Which Car Buying Guide'. This magazine, which is available at most book and magazine shops, gives comprehensive and unreserved individual reports on most types of car. It's a very handy little publication and should be bought and referred to before you go out and shop around. It's quite cheap, so take it, together with this book, and you shouldn't need too much more.

The following notes on makes of car are from my own personal experience. You may know different, or have a friend that does, or disagree or be disappointed with my comments. You may even have, or know of, an example which differs with my conclusions. However, I must say that generally cars follow certain patterns — model, manufacturer and design patterns between countries and regions. These notes are to be used as a rough guide only.

I've pointed out certain cars to be wary of, cars which are of a poor general quality or have specific major design flaws. Others I have suggested that you avoid altogether, those which, in my judgment, are badly made and may give you nothing but a lifetime of trouble. It's also worth reiterating here that there are many cars around which you would be wise to avoid falling in love with. You know which cars those are, they're the ones which make your heart flutter when you look at them. It's all down to personal choice but do remember, never buy a car with anything other than your head.

Alfa Romeo

PROS — Generally spacious, an Italian version of the British mini, a good ride, good handling, pretty tough mechanically, lots of character, the GTV6 is quick and has a fine engine.

CONS — *loads* of rust all over, limited availability of spares and few dealers nationwide. Alfa 33 suffers from noisy and slow-changing gearbox, low resale value on all models, GTV6 has poor gearchange on early models and fast-wearing dampers, Alfa 75 suffers fit and finish problems. Avoid Guiletta.

American Cars

PROS — mechanics and bodywork are built to last (particularly older models) and do not rust easily, loads of goodies (electric everything) which are durable, built for US roads which are generally dreadful and full of potholes. They are, therefore, usually a marvellously smooth ride.

CONS — very high fuel consumption (US fuel prices are a third of the UK's), very limited availability of spares (expensive to buy), left-hand drive models almost without exception.

Aston Martin

PROS — noted for effortless performance, marvellous comfort, dreadfully expensive classic cars, engines extremely durable and reliable, they look and feel terrific, very eye-catching.

CONS — bodyrot in steel under-panels, problems with early fuel injection models, watch for the 'jealous streak' (marks on the body made with screwdrivers or coins by passing envious vandals).

Audi

PROS — German technology, fast, easy to drive fast, reliable, long life.

CONS — pricey spares and service costs, transmission and cylinder head and valve problems after high mileage, early models suffer more rust problems than other German makes, Audi 100 four-cylinder petrol models are too slow. Be wary of Audi 200 turbo.

Austin
PROS — available spares, many good parts can be picked up in scrapyards everywhere quite cheaply.
CONS — not noted for comfort, style or reliability, prone to rust, rapid depreciation. Be wary of Maxi 1500, Ambassador and avoid Allegro and Princess.

Bentley
PROS — marvellous comfort and refinement throughout, highly durable and reliable (see Rolls Royce).
CONS — high petrol consumption, high service and astronomical spares, servicing and insurance costs.

BMW
PROS — German technology, smooth, value for money, performance, tough and long life, great on motorways and ideal for long journeys, look good, status symbol, sophisticated handling, will take a high mileage, well made, lots of electronic goodies to play with.
CONS — high service and parts costs, watch for cars which have been driven hard and fast by boy-racers, electronic problems in some cars, status symbol, watch for slow and imprecise gearchange in 635CSi model, noisy manual gearbox on 7 series models (best buy auto 7's), massive depreciation on newer models.

Chrysler
PROS — available spares, cheap and easy to maintain, lots of room to work around engine.
CONS — poor handling (prone to skidding), bodyrot.

Citroen
PROS — cheap, generally characterful (especially 2CV), great suspension systems, comfortable ride (not 2CV).
CONS — unreliability (especially electrics), noisy gearboxes, pricey spares, clutch cable slip and stick, binding rear brakes, inaccessible mechanics, dealer reluctance to accept as trade-ins.

DAF
PROS — Cheap.
CONS — Uncomfortable, not known for longevity.

Daihatsu
PROS — rough and rugged, last a long time.

CONS — limited availability of spares (though getting better), smoky engines, driven as if a Land Rover but not quite up to it. Avoid Charmont.

Daimler (see Jaguar)

Datsun (see Nissan)

Dutton
PROS — fun summer cars, good roadholding, no rust (fibre glass bodies) cheap sports-looking car, economical, great for sand-dunes etc., for young people only.
CONS — dreadful winter car, noisy cabin and noisy engine (usually Ford Escort — see Ford), cold, awkward to drive, awkward to get in and out of, clumsy looking, clumsily made, poor bodyfit.

Ferrari
PROS — pretty obvious ones, investment potential, very high performance which is better than can be imagined, chassis and mechanics very strong and durable, pedigree, very attractive, great roadholding, catches everyone's eye.
CONS — extremely expensive on parts, spares, service, insurance (you name it), over-inflated prices, rarity (Porsche make more cars per year than Ferrari have ever made), well-disguised crash damage (as Ferraris are *never* written-off and always driven fast).

Fiat
PROS — good positive steering, good steady ride, everyone tells me the X19 will become a classic (but I don't quite believe it).
CONS — pricey spares and service, Panda has timing chain wear and rattle, they don't take to high mileage, flimsy trim, noisy gearboxes, dealer's reluctance to trade-in, slow synchros, creak and rattle in early models, don't hold value, bodyrot. Avoid 126 and Argenta.

Ford
PROS — cheap parts and service, available parts and service, scrapyard availability, generally reasonable economy, a good economical buy, good handling and durable braking systems, older cars (especially estates) hold value reasonably well.
CONS — don't take to high mileage, early Sierras have problems too numerous to mention (so avoid like the plague), clutches wear fast, Escorts develop valve noise, very common cars, smoky engines from

worn valve guides, oil consumption on older engines, watch for ex-boy-racer Capris and amateurishly disguised crash damage. Be wary of Capri 1300 and Cortina 1300 (underpowered).

FSO
PROS — Cheap, cheap, cheap.
CONS — Uncomfortable, poor quality, unreliable.

Hillman
PROS — Scrapyards full of them. Cheap to pick up second hand.
CONS — Rust problems, smoky engine. Be wary of Imp, Avenger and Hunter.

Honda
PROS — good engines, acceptable level of comfort, good supply of spares and easy to service.
CONS — poor damper quality, finishes could be better.

Humber
PROS — Everso-slowly appreciating classic, worth hanging on to, comfortable, refined, attractive.
CONS — watch for big-end wear, dodgy gauges, high petrol consumption.

Isuzu
PROS — elegant, good equipment, durable, good secondhand value for money.
CONS — high insurance costs, scarcity of dealers, low resale value.

Jaguar
PROS — luxury, comfort, easy to drive, handles well, looks good, marvellously comfortable seats, good equipment, noiseless interior, great long-journey car, acceptable number of dealers. Collector's item older models.
CONS — high petrol consumption, costly service and parts, V12 complications (beware), excessive tyre wear, watch for high mileage cars that have been "clocked". Be wary of 2.8 (engine not powerful enough for weight of body).

Lada
PROS — Cheap.
CONS — Extensive rot, extremely low trade-in value, no market for

them, uncomfortable, very basic, unreliable, poorly built, suffers from
a million jokes.

Lancia
PROS — Characterful, stylish, fast, cheap, Monte Carlo rally winner,
appreciating in value and great handling.
CONS — immense amounts of rot all over and all models (not really
built for our weather conditions and salty winter roads), few dealers
nationwide and pricey spares and service costs, poor reliability, rapid
depreciation. Be wary of Trevi.

Lotus
PROS — plastic body (no rot), great driver's car, fair performance —
fastish, British make, available spares and parts, stylish, attractive.
CONS — chassis rot, looks plastic, assembly problems, bumpy ride,
smoky engines from valve guide wear, poor panel fit, poor visibility
in Esprit model, fibre glass crazing.

Mazda
PROS — smooth, later models are reliable.
CONS — early compression sealing and fuel consumption problems,
scarcity of dealers and spares.

Mercedes
PROS — German technology, good value for money, earlier models
provide cheap luxury for any motorist, not bad economy, famously
reliable and marvellously durable, long life, roomy, easy to drive,
always in demand and therefore good resale value, early models
appreciating, beautifully made, solid engines, good paint jobs.
Generally a good buy.
CONS — bulky looking, medium to high fuel economy, high service
costs, pricey parts, not much else.

MG
PROS — light and comfortable steering, easy to resell, MGB sports
becoming collector's item (MGA already is) and fast appreciating
(especially early models).
CONS — poor and noisy gearboxes generally, timing chain problems,
excessive oil consumption, cooling system plagued with problems,
Midgets tend to fall to bits.

Mitsubishi
PROS — reputation for being solid and reliable and strong.
CONS — turbo problems, scarcity of spares.

Morgan
PROS — never loses value, good value for money, looks good, surprisingly economical, engine very good, good back-up service.
CONS — tired ash chassis frame (yes, wooden), problems with crude pillar sliding front suspension, uncomfortable and inconvenient gearchange on some models.

Morris
PROS — workhorse, readily available spares, service easy, mechanical accessibility, Minor is a collector's car, lots of character.
CONS — rot, poor handling, smoky engine (many reasons), oil consumption. Be wary of Marina 1800 TC.

Nissan
PROS — a great reputation for faithful service and reliability, low service cost and good economy, later models have good equipment. Good resale value.
CONS — extremely boring to drive, very plasticy interior, watch for ex-mini-cab cars. Avoid Nissan 300ZX and Cherry.

Opel
PROS — tough, simple mechanics, good long-distance tourer, faithful.
CONS — clutch wear, slow gearbox synchros, binding rear brakes, rear suspension problems, autobox malfunctions, boy-racers cause excessive wear to coupé models.

Peugeot
PROS — good riding, economical, robust.
CONS — basic, noisy engine, poor paint on early cars, rear suspension bush rattles, slow gearbox synchros, dragging clutches. Be wary of 604.

Porsche
PROS — reasonably attractive, German make, tough and strong, turbos offer a lot of performance, uneven pricing (which can be taken advantage of), 928 high performance, 944 not bad either.
CONS — cheaper models very basic inside, oil consumption, crash damage (rarely written-off), excessive prices, high insurance, occasional turbo and gearbox problems, watch for basic models

dressed up as more exotic ones, watch for lack of service history, 924 not really a sports car but probably driven as if it was one.

Range Rover
PROS — The world's ultimate four-wheel drive, reliable, workhorse, ever in demand, good visibility, comfy, fun to drive, robust, very 'county'.
CONS — expensive to buy secondhand, smoky engines, high fuel consumption, bodyrot (not aluminium).

Reliant
PROS — simple, durable, rotproof, economical to the extreme.
CONS — basic, smoky, engine, collapsing trim, electrical problems, hood leaks on SS1, jokes.

Renault
PROS — economical, durable.
CONS — rot, smoky engines, floorpan rust, electrical and instrument failures, low secondhand prices, very poor handling, some scarcity of spares, turbo trouble (overheating problems). Be wary of Fuego Turbo.

Rolls Royce
PROS — too numerous to mention, extreme comfort, best available luxury, no rot, one of the very few cars built to last (lifetime guarantee), good value for money secondhand, silent engines, effortless grace and efficiency.
CONS — Very expensive all round, not easy to insure, status symbol.

Rover
PROS — easy to service, cheapish parts, available parts, luxury available in top models and well worth the extra, the 3.5 litre coupé and saloon a collector's item, the P6 a marvellous powerful machine and reliable.
CONS — fuel pump problems in early models, timing chain rattle in later models, rust in rear subframe, avoid lower cc models (underpowered), 1978-86 models worth little and badly manufactured.

Saab
PROS — very reliable, very solid, well equipped, injected cars perform well.
CONS — turbo trouble on early models (overheating especially), high insurance costs.

Seat
PROS — roomy, Porsche engine, Volkswagon structure, faithful, cheap.
CONS — unreliable, poorly mounted switchgear and instruments in early models, indifferent paint.

Skoda
PROS — good traction on ice and snow, affordable spares, many dealers, cheap new and second-hand value.
CONS — the butt of many jokes, ugly, slow gearbox synchros, clutch wear, sill rust, thin bodies and full of rot.

Subaru
PROS — affordable, estates make the most sense, great reputation for reliability.
CONS — cabins cramped, smoky engines, poor servicing, watch for under-body damage for off-road vehicles (which weren't really made for it).

Talbot
PROS — economical and nippy.
CONS — rust, camshaft problems, suspension rattles. Be wary of Alpine, Sunbeam and Tagora.

Toyota
PROS — smooth, good handling on later models, impressive road performers.
CONS — poor handling on early models.

Triumph
PROS — dependable, strong motorway performance, all TR sports collector's item cars.
CONS — weak transmissions, Stag engines have many problems associated with timing (best with Rover V8 engine substitute). Be wary of TR7 and 2500 PI.

Vauxhall
PROS — simple, light, easy to drive smaller and later models, versatile, reliable, workhorse, faithful, motorway cruiser, easy to work round engines, Cresta becoming collectable.
CONS — rust in floorpans, oil consumption, boring to drive, very common, fast wearing camshaft, auto-transmission malfunctions,

awkward to drive larger models. Avoid Belmont and be wary of 2300 and Firenza.

Volkswagen
PROS — German technology, pedigree, superb reliability, hold value very well, engines last many years and many miles, bodywork durable, chassis sound and very capable, well made, good long-term proposition, economy, very good handling on all models (especialy Golf), very fast GTi, lots of equipment, comfortable, quality paint jobs.
CONS — high servicing and parts costs, disguised body damage on sporty Golfs, boot seal leaks on Jetta model. Be wary of Santana.

Volvo
PROS — extremely safe cars, very solidly built with folding crash zones and roll-bars, very rust resistant, responsive handling, tough, last indefinitely, capable of high mileage, 240/244 the best.
CONS — medium to high fuel consumption (heavy cars), trim problems, stodgy, boring, slow gear synchros on highly used vehicles, automatic transmission problems on early 760 series models.

INDEX

Also in the same series ...

CAR DRIVING IN 2 WEEKS
revised by Andrew M. Hunt

This is accepted as **THE** standard work for Learners, and has helped millions to pass their test. It is continually revised and updated at every reprint so it is full of the latest techniques and information. Over 1¼ million sold!

HIGHWAY CODE QUESTIONS AND ANSWERS
by John Humphries

You *must* know the Highway Code to pass your Test. Your mind is set at rest with 300 questions and answers on the Code, making learning easier and more memorable. In this new edition typical on-the-Test questions are included too.

Now THIS part of the Test won't cause YOU any problems.

TEACH YOUR SON OR DAUGHTER TO DRIVE
by David Hough

Safe handling, full control and confident driving is what this book teaches you. It is achieved by combining the 10 instructive lessons with a working knowledge of the Highway Code.

An ideal companion to *Highway Code Questions and Answers,* and a sure way to become a competent driver.

All uniform with this book

ELLIOT RIGHT WAY BOOKS
KINGSWOOD, SURREY, U.K.

OUR PUBLISHING POLICY

HOW WE CHOOSE

Our policy is to consider every deserving manuscript and we can give special editorial help where an author is an authority on his subject but an inexperienced writer. We are rigorously selective in the choice of books we publish. We set the highest standards of editorial quality and accuracy. This means that a *Paperfront* is easy to understand and delightful to read. Where illustrations are necessary to convey points of detail, these are drawn up by a subject specialist artist from our panel.

HOW WE KEEP PRICES LOW

We aim for the big seller. This enables us to order enormous print runs and achieve the lowest price for you. Unfortunately, this means that you will not find in the *Paperfront* list any titles on obscure subjects of minority interest only. These could not be printed in large enough quantities to be sold for the low price at which we offer this series.

    We sell almost all our *Paperfronts* at the same unit price. This saves a lot of fiddling about in our clerical departments and helps us to give you world-beating value. Under this system, the longer titles are offered at a price which we believe to be unmatched by any publisher in the world.

OUR DISTRIBUTION SYSTEM

Because of the competitive price, and the rapid turnover, *Paperfronts* are possibly the most profitable line a bookseller can handle. They are stocked by the best bookshops all over the world. It may be that your bookseller has run out of stock of a particular title. If so, he can order more from us at any time – we have a fine reputation for "same day" despatch, and we supply any order, however small (even s single copy), to any bookseller who has an account with us. We prefer you to buy from your bookseller, as this reminds him of the strong underlying public demand for *Paperfronts*. Members of the public who live in remote places, or who are housebound, or whose local bokseller is unco-operative, can order direct from us by post.

FREE

If you would like an up-to-date list of all Paperfront titles currently available, send a stamped self-addressed envelope to
ELLIOT RIGHT WAY BOOKS, BRIGHTON RD.,
LOWER KINGSWOOD, SURREY, U.K.